"SUSAN ZIMMER HAS WRITTEN A VERY COMPREHENSIVE AND THOROUGH GUIDE TO THE UNDERSTANDING, PREPARATION AND ENJOYMENT OF COFFEE. LIKE A GRAND COOKBOOK FOR COFFEE LOVERS SUSAN'S BOOK IS A GUIDE FOR THOSE WHO WISH TO MAKE THEIR DAILY ENJOYMENT OF JAVA (COFFEE) AN ADVENTURE IN CULINARY CREATION. TRULY, CAPPUCCINO COCKTAILS IS 'A-WHOLE-LATTE' MORE AND COFFEE'S EXOTIC STORY IS TOLD FROM BEAN TO BLISS."
-SANDY MCALPINE, PRESIDENT, COFFEE ASSOCIATION OF CANADA

"CAPPUCCINO COCKTAILS IS A UNIQUE, FABULOUS COFFEE BOOK OFFERING NEW, ENTICING AND TANTALIZING COFFEE RECIPES. NO COFFEE LOVER OR ESPRESSO MACHINE OWNER SHOULD BE WITHOUT ONE! 'A TOP QUALITY BEAN NEEDS TOP QUALITY PRESENTATION' IS MY MOTTO AND CAPPUCCINO COCKTAILS IS JUST THAT!"
-MARYANN OLETIC, PRESIDENT, www.INNOVATEDPRODUCTSMFG.COM

"SOME BOOKS ARE KNOWN AS COFFEE-TABLE BOOKS AND OTHERS AS BEDSIDE COMPANIONS. SUSAN M. ZIMMER'S WONDERFULLY INVENTIVE, WITTY CAPPUCCINO COCKTAILS IS THE ULTIMATE COFFEE-TABLE RESOURCE BOOK AND AN ALL-DAY COMPANION BOOK. IT'S BRIMFUL OF INTERESTING FACTS AND TEMPTING RECIPES. NO COFFEE CONNOISSEUR SHOULD BE WITHOUT ONE."
-LOUIS B. HOBSON, CALGARY SUN

"CAPPUCCINO COCKTAILS - SPECIALTY COFFEE RECIPES . . . AND 'A-WHOLE-LATTE' MORE IS A VERY INNOVATIVE APPROACH ON RECIPES FOR ONE OF THE MOST POPULAR BEVERAGES IN THE WORLD."
-VIDA RADONOVIC, EDITOR AND CO-PUBLISHER, COFFEE AND BEVERAGE MAGAZINE

Cappuccino Cocktails™

Specialty Coffee Recipes

and 'A-Whole-Latte' more!

A book to enjoy
whether or not you have an Espresso machine,
for
Espresso, coffee and cappuccino aficionados.

——————— Susan M. Zimmer ———————

Cappuccino Cocktails™ Specialty Coffee Recipes
by Susan M. Zimmer.

Copyright© 2001 by Susan M. Zimmer
Published by ESP Publishing Inc.
www.CappuccinoCocktails.com

First Printing – September 2001
Second Printing – June 2002

Cartoonists: Matts Zoumer, Randy Glasbergen, Jared Gonzales
Photographers: Dana Wilson, Ken Anderson, Bud Freud, Laurie Vogt, Thom De Santo, James Fairchild
Editorial: Margo Embury
Text, design & layout: Lee-Anne Rourke: E-mail:jrsmac@cadvision.com
Proofreaders: Michaela and Gerhard Fey

Cappuccino Cocktails™ books may be purchased in bulk orders at special volume
discount prices for fund-raising, sales/business promotions, or educational purposes.
For details call ESP Publishing Inc. at 1-877-888-8898, or visit:
www.CappuccinoCocktails.com

In view of individual complexities and the specific natures of health problems,
the author and publisher expressly disclaim any responsibility for any liability,
loss or risk, personal or otherwise, which is incurred as a consequence,
directly or indirectly, from the use and application of any of the contents of this book.

Canadian Cataloguing in Publication Data

ZIMMER, Susan M.

Cappuccino cocktails
ISBN 0 - 9688048-0-2

1. Cookery (Coffee)   2. Title

Includes bibliographical references and index.

TX817.C6Z55 2000   641.8'77   C00-901480-2

Printed and Produced in Canada
by Centax Books, A Division of PWGroup
Publishing Director – Margo Embury
1150 Eighth Avenue, Regina, Saskatchewan, Canada S4R 1C9
Tel: (306) 525-2304 Fax: (306) 757-2439
Email:centax@printwest.com www.centaxbooks.com

DEDICATION

To my father, ALBERT ZIMMER, who taught me . . .

". . . don't be 50 years old, and wish you had done
something you wanted to do
when you were 40!"

-ALBERT ZIMMER (1923-1978)

Writing creates a sanctuary.
It is a place where friends, although apart, can meet.
-SYLVANA ROSETTI, AUTHOR

ACKNOWLEDGEMENTS

I am blessed and very grateful for my "spirit of significance", Bob Morisset, with whom I share my life. Without his stellar support, eternal optimism, and great patience, this book would have been much more difficult to complete.

This book also acknowledges the first hopeless coffee romantics who combined steamed milk with a cup of Espresso coffee! A special thank you to my Tante Maria and all my loving relatives in Germany, who introduced me to my first Cappuccino Cocktail 35 years ago, and to my loving parents, Rose and Albert, who made those memorable summer holidays in Germany possible.

Through the journey of researching and writing this book I have accumulated an enormous collective debt. "Espresso thanks" to every individual involved in the passions and business of coffee and Espresso. Having had experience in the coffee business for the past 14 years, I would like to thank all my past customers, employers, suppliers and principals for the business opportunities, knowledge and friendships which I have gained. A special thanks to my first foodservice customers, who introduced Cappuccino Cocktails as a promotional menu addition for their restaurants. Also, a special thanks to Chef Beat Hegnauer, for sharing his creative cappuccino cuisine secret with me (us).

This book's eclectic recipes have been creatively designed, customized and collected from various sources over the years; with the assistance of many individuals and the inspiration of others. The very first recipe was "Christmas Cappuccino" in December of 1996. In September 1997, the Cappuccino Cocktails concept, and the inspired recipes, made their debut at the "Taste of Banff". The exciting flavors generated an enthusiastic response from foodservice customers and consumers. I would like to thank my daughter Krista, for her unfailing support and assistance during this initial stage of creating the concept (even though I am certain she sometimes wondered what I was doing and why). Thank you, also, to my daughter Ingrid George, who innocently inspired me to write the, hopefully humorous, "Cowboy Cappuccino" for this book.

I am expressly grateful to the Coffee and Beverage Magazine; Coffee Association of Canada; Freshcup Magazine; Specialty Coffee Association of America; Calgary Herald; Ottawa Citizen; Julia McKinnell/National Post; Jason Osborne/Lite 96 CHFM Radio, for their permissions, submissions and contributions.

To all my great ex-employers and managers, and to the NOT so great ones – to the great ones for allowing me to fly and follow my soaring passions; to the not so great who stressed me out so much I chose to quit and fly wingless into another flight path, towards the "higher grounds". I thank you all for the challenges, obstacles, opportunities and freedom in those experiences. Only by "flying off the cliff" did I realize that the "fear to jump" really does turn into a "freedom flight", and that the obstacles became my opportunities. I grew from my problems' possibilities, which were actually "speed bumps" in my life's path. The coincidences I experienced in my journey have been God's way of being anonymous, for which I am truly grateful.

Two things can happen when you jump off a cliff,
either someone is down below to catch you,
or you learn to grow wings – real fast!

There are others, closer to this book, to whom I also owe an enormous debt of gratitude: Margo Embury, my editor, for her English aptitude, professional and personal care in making this book possible. A special thank you to Lee-Anne Rourke, my computer wizard, for her magical, artistic talents and assistance in the design and layout of this book.

I cherish my best friend Janice DiMillo's first words, when I told her that I wanted to write this book. She shrieked "JUST DO IT!" in her compelling Italian-Polish pitch, as only Janice can do. My dearest cheerleaders – all of my children, Penny Haddad, Sandra Lockhardt, Marina Lawrence, Emily Lawrence, Carol Holz, Barrie Clapson, Heidi Austin, Toni Baccaert, Flo Harris and Margaret Davenport – from my heart "thank you" for being there. To my sister Sonia, whom I unconditionally love for her special caring nature. To Claire Scott, who has been a "Butterfly Blessing" for me, and loving friend. Her second book, "Dare To Dream" inspired me to dream of writing Cappuccino Cocktails the night after I read it – honestly, I truly and actually DREAMT OF IT and I started writing Cappuccino Cocktails the very next day.

A special thank you to the employees at the Office Depot (Macleod Plaza) for their patient and professional assistance for the past 5 years, especially Trevor, Deb and Susan.

The header quote is true, writing this book has created a sanctuary for me. Through its journey I have connected with and have been guided to many wonderful and very special people. I extend a genuine heartfelt thank you to all of you, and if I have failed to mention anyone, please forgive me.

Last but not least, "thank you", the reader – although apart, my friend whom I have not yet met.

With kind and grateful regards,

Susan M. Zimmer.

Susan M. Zimmer

CONTENTS
(Java Jokes and Coffee Quotes "brew" throughout the book!)

CONTENTS

These recipes have been tested in US standard measurements. Common metric measurements are given as a convenience for those who are more familiar with metric. These recipes have not been tested in metric.

The conversation flowed between them
warm and refreshing, like a good cup of coffee.
-Rosamond Lehmann, The Time of Love

LET'S DO COFFEE: AN INTIMATE INTRODUCTION

Drinking coffee and specialty fancy coffees has become a 2.25 billion-cup-per-day lifestyle. The world of coffee employs more than 25 million people around the world to sustain our coffee supply. Whether our beloved brew is purchased from a drive-through kiosk and consumed on-the-go, lingered over in a noisy coffee-pub, or sipped in a cloistered café, specialty coffee consumption has become a distinctive niche in our society.

The emergence of the Espresso era and the cappuccino years have fueled this public phenomenon. An explosion of sophisticated specialty tastes have changed the face of coffee forever. Further expansions of this "new-age beverage culture" have allowed coffee, and all of its variations, to penetrate to many non-traditional venues such as bookstores, gas stations, department stores and airports. In some parts of the country, it seems a coffee bar has sprouted on every street corner.

Specialty coffee beverages have also made huge strides in becoming part of most households. It was only a matter of time before Espresso machines would constitute the spiritual and aesthetic hearts of many North American kitchens. Home Espresso/cappuccino machines are now quickly becoming the kitchen roosters that greet a new morning for many Espresso aficionados. It is estimated that at least 11.6 million households in America already own an Espresso machine, and that 44 percent of them use the appliance frequently.

The best news yet is that you do not necessarily need a special machine to make a creative cappuccino cocktail! If you do own an Espresso machine, that's a bonus. If you do not have one but would prefer to drink Espresso coffee, and your budget cannot accommodate an expensive machine, a stove-top Espresso maker can be purchased for around $20 - $30 at most Italian or kitchen specialty stores. More information is available in the chapter "Coffee Machines and Methods".

In the chapter "Cream of the Cup", we'll get into various tips and methods of steaming and frothing milk for fancy coffees and cappuccino cocktail recipes. "Make a Basic Cappuccino Without a Machine", tips from an Executive Chef, will hopefully inspire you to begin to brew and create cappuccino cocktails today. There is no reason why you cannot perform your own ritual of brewing Espresso and making cappuccino in the comfort of your own kitchen, to please your palate, nourish your soul and entertain your guests.

Cappuccino Cocktails is meant to be a user-friendly recipe and information guide, with easy-to-follow recipes created and collected over my years of coffee and cappuccino experience. Hot and cold specialty coffee concoctions are as varied as the blending combinations of coffee beans. In the flexible recipes which follow, Espresso coffee may be replaced by a dark-roasted or strong coffee, whatever you perceive "strong" coffee to be. Espresso coffee is an acquired taste and many times it is made improperly, leaving the drinker with a bitter taste. Espresso, like coffee, has to be made with love and respect to live up to its aromatic and flavorsome potential. The strength of the coffee, however, is a personal preference, so always suit the coffee strength to your personal palate.

In the recipes to follow, suitable suggested non-alcoholic syrups may be substituted for liqueurs to make non-alcoholic cappuccino cocktails. A complete list of suitable syrups is itemized in the "Coffee Syrups" chapter. Whipped cream, shaved chocolate and maraschino cherries are just a few of the suggested garnishes. Biscotti biscuits or delicious cappuccino/vanilla crème-filled cookie straws make excellent accompaniments to cappuccino cocktails as an after-dinner dessert. With all of these variations available, creating delicious cappuccino cocktail beverages is easy and fun.

One chapter in this book explores "The Wondrous World of Coffee" and another navigates through "A Coffee Atlas", defining the various coffee beans of the world. A historical coffee timeline, "Coffee – Rich In History", takes you through a mosaic of histories dating back over a millennium, offering you insight into the origins and karmic travels of the coffee bean. "Coffee's Future" expands our awareness of the new developments of coffee consciousness from sustainable coffee cultivation to the world's coffee trade. "Coffee and your Health" outlines interesting aspects regarding health effects of this passionately addictive brew. "Coffee Machines and Methods" offers very important tips and information on how to make that perfect brew, including an exclusive section for Espresso coffee making.

Inspiring coffee quotes introduce each chapter and are sprinkled generously throughout the recipes. For common or higher grounds, I hope this book intrigues you with tips 'n' trivia, java jokes, lore and a whole latte more!

So . . . if you are ready to get perking, then grab your beans, read on and let's get brewing.

-Susan M. Zimmer

Here I sit "brewing" Java Jokes, Coffee Quotes
and 'A-Whole-Latte' more!"

-SUSAN M. ZIMMER

"I know life can be a GRIND, 'cause I've BEAN there!"
-SUSAN M. ZIMMER

THE WRITER AND A SOULFUL CUP OF COFFEE

Everyone has a story. Sometimes I feel that my life has been a soap opera. Anyone who knows me could testify to that. Often I have joked about my life, saying "one day, I have to write a book!" Well here it is. A book on coffee? This book is more than just a book on specialty coffee; just like purchasing a pound of coffee is more than just buying coffee beans. The coffee bean's journey of preparation and processing, to reach its brewed destination in your cup, is similar to our life's journey of self-preparation and self-processing. Through each dramatic chapter in my life, it's been both grind and glory to ultimately arrive at the brewing of this book.

Years ago I woke up to smell the latte and realized that everything we experience in life prepares us for where we are in our lives today. Coffee has always been a part of the banquet of my life. I have loved coffee since I was very young, when I discovered decadent Eiskaffees (Iced Coffees) in my Tante (Aunt) Maria's restaurant in Germany, back in the mid-1960s. I patiently had to wait almost 30 years before iced coffee started to become popular in North America. Life can be mysterious and unpredictable; coincidentally I ended up in a selling career for an international coffee company and launched nationally branded hot and cold cappuccino products. From selling commercial coffee, then importing/distributing Espresso machines and specialty coffees, to being an iced cappuccino sales broker, my life has brewed around this beloved bean for the past 14 years. There were a lot of "perks" to selling coffee – what I couldn't sell, I drank!

Recently I took a long coffee break from my laborious life in latteland. I chose to reflect on my "reason for be'an", re-connect, rejuvenate and revive in a coffee communion with my soul. I believe that every experience prepares us for the next one. Inevitably, we live and learn, process and create through the results of our choices in both our personal and professional lives. My life experiences, the good, the bad and the ugly, have been my teachings, for which I have no regrets.

I have measured out my life in coffee spoons . . .
-T.S. ELLIOTT, "THE LOVE SONG OF J. ALFRED PRUFOCK" (1888-1961)

Five years ago, Bob, my soulmate and partner, and I were balancing our own extreme situation, when we chose to blend our families of five teenagers into the Brady Bunch. Through thick and thin, my two children and his three managed to roll with life's punches. Believe me though, some mornings we were brewing more than just hot coffee and frothy steamers! (This was when I began to drink Espresso strong and straight up.) Today, having survived (even thrived), I am blessed with two beautiful granddaughters, Nicola and Anna. I am very proud of all our five children, who have also been stretched, stressed and strengthened from this profound and passionate experience. (Yes . . . Bob is still my best friend.)

He was my cream and I was his coffee and when you poured us together, it was something!

-JOSEPHINE BAKER, DESCRIBING A ROYAL AFFAIR (1906-1975)

Passion is the reason for everything we do and feel. It's a state of mind and being. To get in touch with your passion, you have to somehow find the way back to your heart. So, if you love coffee, grab a cup of your beloved brew and sip your way back to your center. For some people, specialty coffees are at the heart of life's simple indulgences. The coffee revolution has fueled our java passions into a "java joy within". In our society, which is naturally buzzing with over-stimulation, it's ironic that coffee has the capacity to offer dolce niente (the sweetness of doing nothing). It's as if people need to give themselves permission to relax and have a gourmet cup of "I'm worth it". Coffee drinking has always been associated with relaxing and sociability. "Urban social scientists" that is "gourmet city sippers", have claimed that drinking cappuccinos and lattes can "expand the present moment" and can increase the imagination and the "flow experience" (the flow of life and coffee).

Cappuccino Cocktails is a part of my imagination and flow experience. I hope this book will serve as a source for expanded coffee consciousness and a creative recipe guide for your passionate java folks. It has been my pleasure to brew it for you and I hope it inspires you to follow your passion, increase your imagination, and obey your heart's counsel, to wherever life's daily grind may lead you.

Ciao for now.

Take chances and make choices by listening only to your heart's voices.

Then your mistakes are worth making; and the trackless roads are worth taking.

Your passions in life will be what you brew, and by living them to learn . . . the regrets will be few.

-SUSAN M. ZIMMER

ESPRESSO: the ultimate expression of refined living.

-Luigi Lavazza, founder of Lavazza Coffee of Italy

ESPRESSO: EXPRESSIONS OF EXTREME COFFEE

"Espresso" IS . . .

. . . EXTREME COFFEE: The extraction is a precise art form, involving an "interdependence" of factors within the brewing method, including the blend, the roasting, the grind, the proper temperature, the specific pressure and timing – made fresh upon request – one serving at a time.

. . . a powerful main component (or constituent) for cappuccinos, lattes, mochaccinos, café au lait.

. . . where the perfection for any specialty Espresso drink begins!

. . . more than just a beverage, but rather a ritual, an art which changes with every stroke.

. . . a kind of coffee cuisine, a passionate way of experiencing coffee.

. . . the essence of coffee intensified, a deepened coffee consciousness.

. . . una bella tazza di caffe (a beautiful cup of coffee).

. . . a demitasse of intensely rich coffee, made "expressly" for one person.

. . . poco ma buono (small but good).

. . . more so – more aroma, more body, more taste.

. . . the most extreme and extraordinary of beverages.

. . . the aroma of small affordable pleasure.

. . . a potion of enlightenment, where the self-discovery journey can begin – SIT, SMELL, SIP, SILENCE.

. . . a matter of personal preference – choose which Espresso beverage will best complement the present moment.

"Espresso" IS NOT . . .

. . . pronunciated as "EXpresso"!

. . . a paint color, or a modifier to ice cream, tortes or cakes.

. . . a definition for the darkness of a coffee roast.

. . . the degree of fineness of a coffee grind.

. . . a coffee bean, a roast, or specific blend of coffee beans.

. . . a country where coffee is grown!

"Crema" IS . . .

. . . a promise of sweetness, rather than bitterness.

. . . the dark golden "cream" floating enticingly on top of the finished Espresso coffee.

. . . a uniform cream floating on top of the Espresso coffee, free of any white or light brown patches.

. . . the stickiness on the porcelain sides of the Espresso cup, even after the Espresso is consumed.

. . . a thick suspension of microscopic coffee oils and millions of micro gas bubbles.

. . . a rich golden tanned blanket which should NOT dissipate within the first minute of being made.

. . . filled with a full rich aroma, hitting your nose when you "break" up the crema with your first sip.

. . . the nectar of the gods.

ESPRESSO: AN EXTREME DEFINITION

"A true Espresso is produced when $1^1/_2$ oz. (45 mL) of filtered water, at a temperature of 195°F (90°C), passes through $^1/_4$ - $^1/_3$ oz. (7-9 g) of a finely ground quality Espresso coffee, and is forced through the fine coffee grounds at 9 atmospheric pressure (approximately 132 pounds/60 kg per square inch/2.5 cm²), with the water being in direct contact with the coffee for approximately 25 seconds.

"A quality Espresso, when consumed, should leave a pleasant not bitter aftertaste, lingering on the palate for approximately 10 minutes, curling into an almost nutty flavor.

"The 'crema' or 'dark golden cream' crowned on top of the finished Espresso coffee is formed when the emulsified coffee oils are released (due to the high pressure on the grounds) and come into contact with the atmosphere's oxygen. In its buoyant perfection, the crema floats on top of the Espresso coffee."

-SUSAN M. ZIMMER

"Espresso is the dark karmic soul of coffee:
its combinations limitless, its energy timeless,
prepared with passion, pursued with purpose,
it determines its destiny in its next existence."

-SUSAN M. ZIMMER

Toffee Coffee Latte, page 88

Amaretto Mochaccino, page 90

Beans and Machines

"COFFEE BEANS AND MACHINES SHARE CERTAIN
COMMON GROUNDS – FROM CROP TO CUP, THERE'S
A WHOLE WIDE WORLD OF CHOICES!

-Susan M. Zimmer

*Coffee and life share a common ground
— they both offer many choices!*

-SUSAN M. ZIMMER

PART 1
THE WONDROUS WORLD OF COFFEE

A cup of coffee, like any other experience, can be enriched by choices and consciousness. "No beans about it" — the best coffee choices are the ones most
pleasant to your own palate — the selection of one's coffee is a personal
preference.

Choosing coffee beans can be a perplexing experience, since there is a
huge range of coffee types and bean blends from all around the world. The final
coffee flavor and quality involves many complex factors, beginning from the coffee
seed, the beans' botanics, a wide variety of soil and climate conditions, cultivation altitudes, and the care taken in harvesting the beans. Raw green coffee
beans are then subjected to many influencing factors, including: the processing,
production, roasting, blending and brewing methods. On a global note, the
various coffee species and varieties of coffee trees from different areas of the
world also offer their own distinctive flavors.

There are over forty exporting countries; all of which use different classification systems, supplying the world with various coffee bean sizes from sixty
known species of coffee plants. No wonder choosing coffee can involve a puzzling
"java jargon"! Fortunately, the world of coffee nomenclature, from mountain to
market, can be classified into simple basic categories.

The following pages briefly outline the basics of bean botanics, coffee cul-
tivation/processing, global classification used by the coffee trade and coffee
producing countries. There is "a whole wide world of beans" out there and the
"Coffee Atlas" will navigate a "java journey" through the quantum increase of
quality coffees around the world. Each coffee will be visited by country, describing
the respective unique flavors of each growing region.

Theoretically, no amount of information can replace the actual art of
tasting coffee, since "the truth is in the cup". However, the more we enrich our
consciousness with coffee knowledge, the wiser our choices become, helping us
to enjoy "a better . . . not bitter cup of coffee"!

Explore now the wondrous world of coffee.

COFFEE BEAN BOTANICS – GENERAL FACTS

- Simply expressed, coffee is a plant.
- The coffee plant is a member of the Rubiacee family (genus coffea) and grows in a narrow sub-tropical "coffee-belt" region that stretches around the world.
- Coffee plants are fruit-bearing shrubs, which can grow to $9^1/2$ to 40 feet (3 to 12 metres). Cultivated plants are pruned to 8 to 10 feet (2.2 to 3 metres) to make harvesting easier.
- The coffee plants first produce delicate clusters of white blossoms which exude a heavy, jasmine-like fragrance. The very short flowering period varies from region to region. Small green coffee cherries then appear and ripen to a bright red as they reach maturity. Within six to nine months they turn almost black, ready to be harvested.
- The soft, yellow flesh of the "cherries" contains two seeds (or coffee berries) covered with a hard protective covering. Inside there is a thin protective (pulp) silvery membrane.
- The size of the beans differs in each of the 60 known species of coffee plants.
- The three best-known species of coffee grown commercially, each with its own varieties, are coffea arabica, coffea robusta and coffea liberica.

ARABICA BEANS

- Arabica, the "aristocrats" of coffee beans, are grown at the highest altitudes and are the most prized beans, demanding the highest prices in the world. They are the only beans used by the finest specialty coffee roasters, and are responsible for a coffee's aroma, body and smoothness.
- Arabica is the most widely cultivated bean, constituting 75 percent of the world's coffee production.
- Arabica coffee beans do best at altitudes of 3,000 to 6,500 feet (900 to 2,000 metres), where the slower-growing process concentrates their flavors into a richer, more refined body flavor. The higher the altitude where the arabica beans are grown, the finer the quality of the harvested beans.
- These beans need soil that is rich in minerals, and a constant temperature of about 68°F (20°C). They require very careful cultivation, with just the right climactic conditions, and they are susceptible to disease, frost and drought.
- Arabica shrubs yield 1 to $1^1/2$ pounds (500 to 700 grams) of green coffee per shrub per year.
- Arabica coffee beans contain about 1 percent caffeine by weight.

ROBUSTA BEANS

- This coffee bean species is used for the lower grades of coffee sold throughout the world.
- This species does best at lower altitudes and elevations, even on plains, where the climate is unsuitable for the arabica species. It will do well even in poor growing conditions.
- Coffea robusta is very hardy and disease resistant.
- Robusta demands the lowest prices in the world, and becomes anonymous when used in lower-priced commercial coffee blends and soluble instant coffees. The robusta is responsible for the strength and intensity in a finished cup of coffee.
- Robusta shrubs have a higher yield than arabica, about 2 to 3 pounds (1 to 1.5 kilograms) of green coffee per shrub per year.
- Robusta coffee beans contain about 2 percent caffeine by weight.

LIBERICA BEANS

- This coffee bean species is the third most recognized commercial variety. This species is similar to the robusta in that it also grows better at lower altitudes. It is hardy and can withstand poorer climate conditions.
- It is a minor crop from Africa.

These beans are my sole sustenance.
They come from the berries on the hillsides.
-SHEIKH OMAR, TO THE CITIZENS OF MOCHA, YEMEN (AD 1258)

COFFEE BEAN CULTIVATION AND PROCESSING

Coffee production requires a great deal of human effort, from "the coffee crop to the last drop!" From the prudent planting of the trees to the painstaking picking of the cherries; from the washing, drying, sizing, to the sorting, grading and selecting, the delicate coffee beans rarely leave the touch of human hands. To value a cup of coffee, is to respect the labor of love required – the caring human effort which was put into producing it.

COFFEE BEAN PLANTING

- The most favorable seedbeds for the cultivation of coffee are soils which are volcanic in origin and rich in nitrogen.
- The optimum climate conditions are those prevailing in the tropics, where temperatures remain between 59 to 77°F (15 to 25°C). Wind, frost, leaf disease, and even excessive heat, will destroy the shrubs.
- Plenty of rain, in combination with alternating dry periods, will produce the best crops.
- Carefully selected seeds are sown into suitable, prepared seedbeds.
- Slender shoots sprout up in eight weeks. After one year the young plants are transplanted to permanent coffee plantation sites.
- Young plants do not bear fruit (coffee seeds) for the first two years; however, they still require great care in hoeing, weeding, pruning and frequent watering to ensure proper growth.
- The plants begin their productive life span of about 15 to 20 years after their first flowering (coffee seeds), giving an annual yield of 1 to 2 pounds (500 to 900 grams) of coffee per plant per year.
- When the coffee plant's white delicate flowers blossom, the orange and jasmine-like fragrance is as intoxicating as the flowers are beautiful; however, the blossoms are short-lived, only two to three days. Clusters of green "cherries" (coffee berries) appear, turning yellow, red and then a deep crimson color. When the cherries are almost black, they are ready to be harvested.

The coffee farmers in Jamaica are signaled by "bats" as to when to begin harvesting their crop. When the bats start their nightly sucking on the sweet pulp of the cherries, this signals the farmers to begin!

BEAN HARVESTING: PICKING AND STRIPPING

The harvesting period varies from region to region, coffee tree to coffee tree, because not all of the coffee cherries ripen to maturity at the same time. This can take several weeks and consume tremendous labor costs. There are two systems employed in harvesting: "picking" and "stripping".

- Picking ensures a perfectly uniform, top-quality harvest, as trained pickers expertly pick only mature cherries – one by one. Pickers of quality coffees must return to the same tree time after time, to pick more cherries as they ripen.
- Stripping is used in some countries, where plantations are vast and labor costs are high. This economical, labor-saving method is definitely faster; however, it results in a harvest of lesser-quality beans, since unripe and over-ripe cherries are savagely plucked by machines, along with the mature ones. The harvest is usually infested with all sorts of impurities, such as leaves, stones, unripe and rotten berries.

Once the cherries are harvested, they are transported for coffee bean preparation and processing.

COFFEE BEAN PREPARATION AND PROCESSING

In preparing the green coffee beans for market, they have to be removed from the husk or pulp of the cherries which were picked off the coffee shrubs. There are two methods of removing these outer layers to get to the coffee beans inside: "wet" and "dry". In both methods of separating the pulp or husks from the coffee beans, the beans are sifted through various sizes of screens, and then graded and sorted by size, ALL BY HUMAN HANDS!

THE "WET" METHOD:

- This method is considered to produce "the better bean". It is used for the hand-picked, quality beans.
- With this method, the coffee beans must be extracted from the freshly harvested "cherries" within 24 hours. The pulp which protectively surrounds the precious coffee beans is removed by: cleaning the cherries, removing the husk or pulp, steeping in fermentation tanks, washing and, finally, drying the beans.
- Contrary to how it sounds, the fermentation stage gives the beans a superior flavor.
- Sometimes coffees made from beans prepared by this method are referred to as "washed coffees", due to the beneficial soaking the beans get.

THE "DRY" METHOD:

- This method of removing the outer layers of pulp to get to the coffee beans is sometimes referred to as the "natural" method.
- The picked cherries are spread in thin layers and dried in the sun or in dryers. The pulp of the cherries is then separated from the coffee by a mechanical husker.

Beauty is in the hand of the bean-holder!

COFFEE BEAN SORTING AND GRADING

The sorting of the beans can be performed by hand, by machine, or a combination of both. The hawk-eyed humans with nimble hands, however are capable of removing unwanted materials such as stones, immature beans, twigs and leaves. The more detail given to the cleaning and sorting process, the better the quality of the finished beans and the higher the prices they can command.

The grading of the beans appoints value to various coffees for international trading purposes. It is the ultimate of a sophisticated sorting system and a device to control an agricultural commodity. Coffee grading terminology can become a language of its own. It distinguishes one coffee-producing country from another, pertaining to certain coffee bean criteria, such as:

- imperfections of the harvest such as broken, immature beans, the presence of sticks, stones, leaves, etc.
- size of the bean (the bigger the better)
- age of the crop (how old the coffee shrubs are from which the beans were harvested)
- the altitude where the coffee crop was grown (the higher the better)
- the processing method used (wet or dry method)
- species and variety of the plant (arabica, robusta, and then what variety of that species)
- plantation or area of production (this gives the region a signature market name)
- cup quality (a criterion based simply on how good the coffee tastes and smells)

After grading, the green coffee beans are packed in the standard 132-pound (60 kilogram) burlap coffee sacks, for shipment to roasters in consumer countries all around the world.

These berries are the devil's work!
So back to the devil these fruits must go!
-ANGRY MOSLEM IMAM, ROASTING THE FIRST COFFEE BEANS (AD 850)

COFFEE ROASTING CHEMISTRY

Nothing affects coffee flavor more than how the green "raw" beans have been roasted. If you were to brew raw beans, there would not be any recognizable coffee flavors. Roasting is the key stage, where the characteristic taste, aroma, and final flavor of the beans is developed. The "length of time" of the roasting process also determines whether the coffee will end up being a Cinnamon, City, Espresso, or Dark French roast. In simplified terms, coffee is described as "light", "medium" or "dark" roasted.

- In the roasting process, heat from an external source is applied to the raw coffee beans in large vats or drums, spinning and heating them evenly at temperatures reaching up to 550°F (290°C). The heat essentially creates chemical changes in the physical structure and composition of the beans.
- Water evaporates from the beans; starches convert to sugars; and the sugars caramelize. The beans increase in size by about 25 to 35 percent. The beans begin to pop, much like popcorn. They lose about 18 to 22 percent of their weight, mostly through evaporation. (The caffeine content, however, is not affected by these changes).
- Gradually, the green beans turn a yellowish color, then darken into a deep rich brown. During this color change, a number of chemical reactions occur, causing the beans' sugars and proteins to interact with each other. It is these changes, and the release of caffeol or coffee oils, that are essential in bringing out the flavor and aroma of the beans. The darker the beans the more coffee oils they form.
- It is the length of the roasting time and the temperature of the process which determines the fullness of the flavor, acidity, aroma and depth of color of the beans. Great care must be taken as the process nears completion to ensure that the beans are not burnt.

MY PERSONAL FAVORITE:

The best Espresso coffee I have ever tasted was one which had been "air-roasted", whereby the beans were actually floating to roasting perfection in a super-heated pressurized airstream within a roasting drum. The coffee beans never touch the scorching metal walls of the roasting drums. In many roasting facilities, gravity pulls the coffee beans to the bottom of the metal drums, where they become burnt, blackened and bitter. This burnt flavor is evident in the final brew. An excellent Espresso should never be bitter, if it is, you can be sure it was primarily due to overroasting or poor roasting methods.

- Flavorful acids form as the beans turn into a medium-dark roast. As the roasting progresses, however, into a darker roast, the same acids will now begin to break down and the sugar components begin to caramelize, which lends body and the mouth-feel texture of a darker roast. That is why Espresso coffee beans are characteristically low in acidity, rich in body and sometimes caramelly.
- After this monitored roasting process, the coffee beans are rapidly cooled down by jets of cold air, thereby sealing in all the flavor and aroma which the heated air has brought to life from the dormant green beans.

COFFEE ROASTING CHART

LIGHT	MEDIUM	MEDIUM DARK	DARK	DARKER	VERY DARK
Cinnamon	American	Full City	Italian	Espresso	Dark French
New England	Med. Brown	Vienna	Espresso	Italian	French
Light	Brown	Velvet	European	Continental	Italian

- The lighter the roast the more flavor acids; interesting life and sparkle; lighter in body because the light roast lack caramelized sugars; dryer beans.
- The medium roasts have less acidic snap; richer and more rounded flavor. At the darker roast stage the coffee oils begin to appear.
- At the dark roast stage all acidic tones disappear; beans are oilier; a definite bittersweet, chocolatey flavor; rich and full in body and texture.
- An interesting note on caffeine content and roasting – the darker the roast, the less caffeine content it will have. The higher roasting temperatures eliminate more of the caffeine in the beans.

"THE ALTERNATIVE": ROAST YOUR OWN AT HOME

Many coffee aficionados all over the world roast their own coffee to enjoy the ultimate in the satisfaction of ritual and the freshest cup of coffee possible. For people concerned about the environment, back to nature and country-life folks, home roasting is ideal! Purchasing a big sack of green raw coffee beans is certainly more economical, and one can curb the cans, waste and processing expense.

Nowadays, there are very good electric home-roasting machines, but the "back-to-basics" of roasting are simply: "skillet-on-top-of-the-stove" or the old "skillet-in-the-oven" methods. The physical requirements of both these approaches are also simple: the raw green coffee beans need to be kept moving in temperatures of at least 400°F (200°C) and, secondly, they have to be cooled down at the precise moment of the desired degree of roast. The quicker the roast, the better the coffee!

"SKILLET-ON-THE-STOVE" ROAST YOUR OWN METHOD:

- Using an old heavy (metal) handled frying pan (with cover), spread only one layer of green coffee beans at a time into the pan. (An aluminum egg poacher pan is ideal!)
- Place an inexpensive oven thermometer in the pan. (Ideally, one with a flat metal back which can be laid on an angle in the pan. This can then register the air in the pan rather than the temperature of the bottom surface of the pan.)
- Begin with medium heat and raise the heat until the thermometer registers 500°F (260°C), then turn the heat down to steady the temperature at around 400°F (200°C). Peek at the thermometer once in a while to be certain 400°F (200°C) is being maintained.
- Holding the cover, begin to gently shake the beans in the pan, at one-minute intervals, to roast the beans evenly.
- The beans will begin to snap crackle and pop! (Smoke will start to seep out so make sure the windows are open and the stove's air ventilator is on.) The beans will begin to change color, first becoming a yellowish-brown, then swelling and darkening. Watch the color, and stop just before the desired degree of roasting has been achieved.
- It is important to never let the beans darken to more than a chocolate brown color.
- Once the desired roasting has been reached, remove pan from heat and dump the beans into another, cool, pan or onto slate or marble. The quick cool down will close the bean pores to preserve the coffee's aroma.

"SKILLET-IN-THE-OVEN" ROAST YOUR OWN METHOD:

• Preheat oven to 500°F (260°C). Spread an even layer of beans (1/2 inch/1.3 cm) in an old iron frying pan and place in a preheated oven. Shake the pan occasionally during the entire 20-minute roasting time, for a mild to medium roast. For a higher roast, reduce the heat to 400°F (200°C) after 20 minutes, and continue roasting for another 20 minutes (maximum), stirring occasionally.

A NOTE ON POPCORN (COFFEE BEAN) POPPERS:

• These neat stove-top pans can double as coffee roasters. Many kitchen boutiques sell them, retailing from about $15 to $30.
• An oven thermometer is needed to establish the proper temperature (as noted above) before the beans are cranked around in the pot.

> *All of life is a dispute over taste and of tasting.*
> -FRIEDRICH NIETZSCHE, GERMAN PHILOSOPHER (1844-1900)

"CUPPING": COFFEE CUP-TESTING

Expert coffee-tasters are the aristocrats of the coffee industry. These coffee masters specialize in tasting small samples of various coffee beans, which are considered for future coffee markets. Professional coffee-tasting is referred to as "cupping". It is similar to wine-tasting, in that these experts can distinguish the very origin in a sample coffee blend, simply by smelling and tasting. These taste differentials are detected on a coffee-educated palate as clearly as salt and sugar. There are, however, very few individual who possess this rare ability. In fact the New York Coffee and Sugar Exchange employs under 40 tasters responsible for all the coffee imported for the entire United States market.

Objective and scientific notes are kept on the impressions of each coffee bean sample, using all five senses to objectively assess the coffee, based on:

• Presentation
• Sight
• Aroma
• Taste
• Body
• Acidity

Professional coffee tasters are passionate about their special abilities. They slurp the coffee violently and noisily from a testing spoon. The coffee being sampled is almost inhaled into the back of the mouth and sprayed on the roof of the palate, then rolled and almost chewed before it is professionally spit into a bucket!

This tasting exercise is certainly NOT part of my after-dinner etiquette! I tend to smell and taste my coffee or cappuccino and drink it with grateful acknowledgement to the coffee aristocrats at the top of the coffee industry lineup!

How do I drink thee? Let me count the ways.
I drink thee for the taste and scent and roast.
My senses feel . . . the memories of coffee nights and days.

-ELIZABETH BARRETT ROASTING (NEE BROWNING), L'ENVOI

COFFEE BLENDING CHEMISTRY

Blending various types of coffees is an art. Each blend is the official signature of the inspired coffee roaster. Roasters, specialty coffee shops, office coffee services and foodservice companies usually offer their secret "house blends". Countless coffee creations are made world-wide by combining coffees which complement one another with qualities the other lacks.

One of the principle arts of blending coffees is balancing the extremes of the coffee types being used, so that no two coffees are blended which possess the same extremes in the same way. For example, if both coffees are sharp and winey, such as an Ethiopian and a Kenyan, then these two would not marry well. On the other side of the cup, the most famous blend, Arabian Mocha and Java, each offer distinctive extreme qualities, and together produce a balanced rich, flavorful cup of coffee. The Arabian Mocha's mild acidity and light body couples well with the Java's heavy body and deep-toned flavors.

COFFEE-BLEND PARTNERSHIPS WHICH HAVE CEMENTED TRADITIONS OVER THE YEARS:

Mocha and Java – a traditional favorite
Mocha and Mysore – a Turkish coffee favorite
Brazilian Santos and Ethiopian Harrar – a Neopolitan favorite
Mocha and Sumatra – known to be rich and strong
Brazilian Bourbon Santos and Colombian Bogota
Costa Rican, Sumatran and Hawaii
Kenyan, Mocha and Guatemalan
Brazilian Arabica, Robusta and Ethiopian – popular in Greece

RECOMMENDATIONS FOR BLENDING ONE EXTREME COFFEE PERSONALITY WITH ANOTHER WHICH COMPLEMENTS IT:

For body and richness: add Sumatran Mandheling, Celebes Kalossi or Java
For sweetness: add Venezuelan Maracaibo or Haitian
For even more sweetness, or to even out a bright acidic coffee: add Mysore
For flavor and aroma: add Kona, Sumatran, Celebes, Guatemalan, Colombian or Jamaican Blue Mountain
For a winey note: add Ethiopian and Kenya or Mocha for extra richness
For brightness, acidity and snap: add a good quality Central American such as Costa Rican or Guatemalan

Too bad we don't have such a guide to follow for our own marriages!

When ordinary coffee just won't do . . .

FLAVORED COFFEE BEANS

Flavoring coffee is as old as the beverage itself. The Arabs were the first coffee connoisseurs to add spices such as cinnamon to their beloved brew. Middle Easteners followed with the addition of cardamom, cloves, nutmeg, allspice and even ground nuts. Spirits, chocolate and citrus peels were also added later on. Once coffee was introduced to the Western world, the now traditional cream and sugar were added to coffee.

Flavored whole-bean coffees have made a fragrant appearance in specialty coffee shops and in the local supermarket's bulk bins since the early 1980s. The variety of flavored coffees is amazing, with the biggest sellers being French Vanilla, Irish crème, hazelnut, macadamia nut, chocolate and spice-based flavors.

These assertive aromas come from adding artificial flavoring agents to the whole coffee bean during the roasting process, sometimes leaving a distinct chemical aftertaste. There are, however, natural flavored coffees available which are essentially extracts in an alcohol and water or glycerine base. Some flavored coffee fans enjoy adding the flavorings, in the way of syrups, to the coffee after it has been brewed. The Italians were known for their variety of fountain syrups, and it was only a matter of time before the syrups found their way into coffee drinks. For more information on flavored syrups see page 148.

SPECIALTY COFFEE VS. COMMERCIAL COFFEE

SPECIALTY COFFEE:

- These are the legal terms used in the coffee trade for signature roasted coffees produced in smaller scale facilities, by private corporations.
- They are generally sold locally and possess a signature personality of their own.
- Specialty coffees have inspired a distinct common-ground culture for coffee connoisseurs, and are in a specialized niche, offering a wide variety of coffee choices which must be notable in quality.
- Specialty coffee beans are always well prepared, freshly roasted and properly brewed.
- Specialty coffees offer superb sensuous qualities of aroma, flavor and esthetic satisfaction.

COMMERCIAL COFFEE:

- These are usually roasted, produced and packed in enormous plants, under nationally branded names, advertised ferociously, and distributed nationally and regionally.
- Commercial coffees are part of the organized retail food distribution network and focused to sell to the mass consumer.
- Commercial coffees offer a very limited selection of blends and roasts. They restrict the coffee connoisseur from experimenting with various coffee blending creations.

You can grind my coffee any time!

-BESSIE SMITH (1894-1937)

GRINDING AND STORING COFFEE – A MATTER OF FRESHNESS

Grinding coffee is a matter of freshness! Fascinating facts on coffee freshness:

Green raw coffee beans:	retain their freshness for years,
Roasted coffee:	begins to lose its flavor after a week,
Ground coffee:	within an hour after grinding it,
Brewed coffee:	within minutes!

Regardless of modern packing technologies, once a consumer opens a canned or packaged prepack of ground coffee, the relatively fresh coffee begins to lose its aroma and freshness due to oxidation. Oxygen, heat and light are true curses to coffee, causing the delicate aromatic coffee oils to deteriorate. Coffee also acts as a sponge, absorbing other aromas. For example, as when smelling and sampling various perfumes at cosmetic counters, inhaling the aroma of coffee beans is suggested in order to neutralize all the other fragrant aromas. I can also remember my mother placing a cup of ground coffee in the refrigerator to absorb unpleasant odors.

The first solution to freshness is to purchase bulk coffee beans in smaller quantities and grind the beans just before brewing the coffee. The Arabs still have the best solution: roast, grind, brew and drink the coffee all in the same sitting! Although this is not always possible, at least grinding your own beans can certainly offer a fresher cup of coffee than having your coffee preground at the store. Pregrinding is just a way of ensuring stale coffee. Grinding our way to a fresher cup of coffee brings us to the following facts, different grinds are required for different brews!

If you brew your coffee the slower way – more coarse coffee it takes;
Fewer beans for the finer way – then quicker coffee it makes.

Ground coffee from a grinding machine
Must match both brew pot and, of course, the coffee bean!

In grinding your beans you will quickly find,
Coffee flavor so fresh – it won't be a grind!

-SUSAN M. ZIMMER

Tired of the Same Old Grind?
Here's the Deal – Tailor the Grind to Suit the Brew Pot!

Different coffee brewing methods require different types of coffee grinds and different grinds require different lengths of brewing time.

The shorter the brewing time, the finer the coffee grind must be, as with making an Espresso! The finer the grind, the less you need. With a finer grind there is more surface area of coffee for the water to infuse. The increased exposure of the grind's precious aromatic oils produces a more intense coffee. (In this case, less is more!)

Conversely, the longer the brewing contact time, the coarser the grind must be (like the French-press or plunger pot method). Coarser grinds require longer brewing cycles, where the coffee grounds steep in the water (as tea leaves do). If, for example, finely ground coffee is used for a plunger pot method, then the brewed coffee will be over-extracted and bitter. Similarly, if a coarse grind is used to make an Espresso, the coffee will be weak.

A GENERAL BREWING GUIDE FOR VARIOUS GRINDS:

Extra-fine grind — up to 30 seconds brewing time
Fine grind — 1 to 4 minutes brewing time
Medium grind — 4 to 6 minutes brewing time
Coarse grind — 6 to 8 minutes brewing time

Real cowboys grind coffee beans with their teeth!
-Susan M. Zimmer

COFFEE GRINDING GUIDE

This grinding guide is based on using an average propeller grinder with no more than 4 scoops/$\frac{1}{4}$ cup (125 mL) at a time. Cut down on the grinding time for quantities less than 4 scoops. Please keep in mind that both the machine and the person operating them can vary.

Cowboy, Open pot or hobo:
Grind type: very coarse or cracked beans with a wide range of sizes.
(If you are a cowboy grind 10-15 coffee beans per mouthful for up to 4 seconds!)

French press or plunger pot:
Grind type: medium to coarse (like bread crumbs). Should feel like coarse sandpaper or cornmeal to touch.
Grinding time: 10-15 seconds

Vacuum pot:
Grind type: medium grit, with little powder.
Grinding time: 15 seconds

Metal filter drip or flip-drip (napoletana):
Grind type: medium to coarse with no powder present.
Grinding time: 15 seconds

Paper filter drip:
Grind type: medium grind with no powder present. Just a touch finer than the metal filter drip grind.
Grinding time: 16 seconds

Stovetop Espresso Moka pot:
Grind type: medium to fine grind, like fine sand.
Grinding time: 20 seconds

Electric pump Espresso machines: (these machines require fine consistent grinds)
Grind type: very fine. It should have a texture between flour and table salt.
Grinding time with an expensive home burr mill: 20-25 seconds

Middle Eastern or Turkish Method:
Grind type: the finest of the finest. It should feel as soft as flannel, with the texture of flour. You may want to purchase this type of coffee in a specialty coffee shop!

GRINDERS AT A GLANCE

Grinding your coffee fresh from whole beans takes very little time, and it is inexpensive. It allows you to grind the beans in a way that accentuates what you like in a coffee, and what works best with your personal brewing method. From the sophisticated quickie electric methods to the manual mortar and pestle, you will experience the full aroma of your coffee, since whole beans retain the rich fragrance that gives coffee its flavor and aroma.

BURR MILL (manual or automatic) or milling-style coffee grinders produce an important evenness to the grind for a more uniform brew. The electric household models are great for quick and easy grinding. The cleanup is relatively easy and the upgraded models offer an automatic timing device for lazy perfectionists.

BLADE-STYLE ELECTRIC coffee grinders use a small, electric motor to spin two metal blades at very high speeds, chopping and crushing the coffee beans. One disadvantage is that the blade grinder must repeatedly slice the bean, and this repeated contact can eventually heat the beans and damage their flavor. To prevent this, it is recommended grinding the beans in short bursts of 3 to 5 seconds at a time, to keep the blades form "burning the beans" and produce a more uniform grind.

BOX GRINDERS are sometimes wooden hand-held propeller models. The beans are simply fed into a little door in the top of the box, and the ground coffee falls into a little bottom drawer. These are great, except for achieving fine grinds and for grinding larger quantities of coffee. Certain upgraded models are available, which can be mounted on a wall or table. These can achieve a finer grind.

MANUAL MORTAR AND PESTLE is the most primitive approach to grinding coffee beans, in fact, it is still used by some Arabs today! This time-consuming technique is all done by hand, it builds strong muscles, but it is difficult to achieve an even coffee grind! If you love to make your own pesto or crush fresh basil with olive oil, then this will be the most esthetically satisfying for you. (Just be careful not to produce coffee-flavored pesto!)

A PURPOSE FOR COMMON GROUNDS:

- The common and most important goal in all of these grinding methods is to achieve an even, uniform grind to provide an even extraction of the oils from the coffee.
- Uneven ill-proportioned grinds can taint the taste of even the finest of beans.
- Uneven coffee grinds will cause some of the coffee to over extract and some to under extract.
- Over-extracted coffee tastes bitter and overly pungent.
- Under-extracted coffee tastes weak, thin and lifeless.

Coffee is a living organism.
It breathes oxygen and releases carbon dioxide.
-SUSAN M. ZIMMER

STORAGE TIPS

Coffee does breathe. The trick to keeping it fresh is to prevent the coffee from being exposed to oxygen. Sometimes whole coffee beans can be purchased in "valve lock bags" which do not allow oxygen to enter the coffee bag, but allows the coffee's carbon dioxide to be released. As soon as you break the seal, however, you will need a proper container (as outlined below) in which to store the remaining coffee. Following are a few tips for storing coffee.

- Always store coffee away from its enemies: light, heat, oxygen, humidity.
- Purchasing coffee in whole beans and grinding your own allows the coffee to stay fresher longer as there is less surface area exposed to air and moisture during storage.
- If possible, purchase only a week's worth of coffee (beans) at a time and store (ground or whole) coffee in an airtight, opaque canister (to prevent light from coming through).
- Ceramic canisters with metal rings that latch shut are also ideal containers for coffee since they cannot transfer any contaminants to the coffee.
- Never use a plastic or metal container since they allow a fair amount of flavor migration and penetration which will corrupt the coffee.
- An odd tip, but it works: cut a green garbage bag into squares, just large enough to line the inside of your coffee container. Store the coffee inside this bag, and seal the top of the green plastic with an elastic band. Keep this bag of beans or grounds "inside" the coffee storage container. The garbage bag material is ideal for preventing light, heat and moisture from robbing the precious coffee aromas and preventing the coffee oils from going rancid. It adds extra protection inside the container.
- The storage container should be just big enough for the quantity of coffee to be stored, to prevent as little air (oxygen) at the top of container as possible.
- Keep beans whole until you are ready to grind; then brew the coffee.
- Only whole beans should be stored in the freezer, preferably in one-week-usage packages.
- Never store coffee in the refrigerator. The coffee can absorb unpleasant odors and the temperature is not ideal.
- Ground coffee can also absorb freezer odors. The coffee oils, especially in darker roasted coffee beans, such as Espresso beans, congeal when frozen, changing the consistency and harming the body of the brewed coffee.

Way down among Brazilians
Coffee beans grow by the billions
So they've got to find those extra cups to fill
They've got an awful lot of coffee in Brazil.
-FRANK SINATRA, THE COFFEE SONG (1946)

PART 2
COFFEE-PRODUCING COUNTRIES

Situated between the Tropics of Cancer and Capricorn, where the climate is hot and humid, lie four geographic regions: *South America, Central America and the Caribbean, Asia and Africa.* Within these regions lie the coffee-producing countries, supplying the world with an annual production of about 91 million sacks, each weighing an average of 132 pounds (60 kilos)!

South/Central America produces:	70 percent of the world's coffee supply
Asia and Indonesia produces:	20 percent of the world's coffee supply
Africa produces:	10 percent of the world's coffee supply

Of the worldwide coffee market, arabica coffee beans account for 75 to 80 percent: robusta beans account for the remaining 20 to 25 percent.

SOUTH/CENTRAL AMERICA

Ol' blue eyes wasn't just singing sweet dixie when he sang about the *coffee beans in Brazil growing by the billions!* Brazil is by far the world's leading coffee producer, supplying mainly high-quality natural arabicas, followed by Columbia, Venezuela, Peru and Ecuador which supply washed arabicas. Brazil is also the second-largest producer of robusta coffees, after Indonesia. A single component, for example, is the massive Brazilian coffee grower, *Ipanema Agro Industria, the world's largest "single" coffee grower.* The 12.4 million coffee trees planted on 12,350 acres (123.5 hectares) of land produce, on the average, 15,000,000 pounds (6,810,000 kilos) of green coffee in one good harvest year! This output from a single Brazilian coffee grower is nearly twice the supply of Jamaica and Hawaii combined!!

Coffee production plays a strategic role in the economy of Mexico, Panama and the islands of the Caribbean. Their coffee products, which are primarily washed arabicas are generally very high in quality.

ASIA AND INDONESIA

India and Indonesia have adopted modern growing methods over the years, thereby increasing their coffee supply of washed arabicas, as well as washed and natural robustas, to the world.

AFRICA

This continent, being located in the heart of the hottest tropical areas of the world, produces primarily robusta coffee beans. In the higher altitudes of Kenya and Tanzania, the arabica coffee bean grows very well, yielding large quantities of washed arabicas.

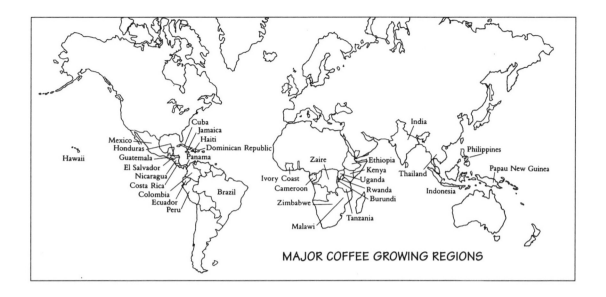

MAJOR COFFEE GROWING REGIONS

GLOBAL COFFEE CLASSIFICATIONS
– COMMODITY TRADING TERMS

Let's go global for an international translation of coffee trading terms (not to add to any more coffee confusion!). The coffees of the world are divided into three general categories for commodity world trading. These three basic coffee categories, the milds, brazils and robustas, are used in discussions of coffee blending and sometimes for Espresso cuisine.

MILDS

High-grown "milds" include all the arabica species grown at altitudes of over 2,000 feet (610 metres) above sea level, usually 4,000 to 6,000 feet (1,200 to 1,830 metres), from anywhere in the world! Only these finest "milds" are purchased for specialty coffee roasting, demanding the highest prices on the world market. These "milds" grow best in well-watered, mountainous regions of the tropics. They are produced only from ripe coffee berries, picked and prepared with the ultimate care.

BRAZILS

The second preferred group of coffees on the global scale, referred to by the trade name "Brazils", is a lower-grade coffee which is mass harvested and grown at lower altitudes on massive plantations. These coffees have an average neutral flavor and a flat aroma. These include all of the coffees grown in Brazil, all of which are lower-grade arabicas, since they are usually strip-picked and carelessly processed.

ROBUSTAS

Even though the third group, robustas, is known for its intensity, inferior quality and higher caffeine content than the "milds", they have inadvertently grown to a role of major importance in world markets. Their main advantage over the milds is that they are very hardy, resistant to diseases, and grow successfully, in higher yields, on lower altitudes than the related arabicas. Robustas demand the lowest prices in the international trading markets, thereby making this group an attractive commodity for the mass-produced commercial supermarket brands and instant coffees, where their inferior qualities become anonymous.

A COFFEE ATLAS – COFFEE SPECIES FROM AROUND THE WORLD

ARABIA (See YEMEN)

BRAZIL (Coffee species: *Santos, Bourbon Santos, Rio, Paran, Victoria, Bahia*)
- Brazil represents quantity of beans rather than bean quality.
- Brazil is of supreme importance as a giant supplier for the commercial coffee industry; however, for the specialty coffee industry its ranking is low.
- The milder *Santos* species is the most popular, of which the smooth *Bourbon Santos* is the highest-grade coffee Brazil produces. It is usually sold as "Brazilian" coffee in the supermarkets, and exhibits a medium body with moderate acidity.
- As for the rest of the bean species: *Rio, Parana, Victoria, Bahia*, the Brazilian coffee industry specializes in producing "price-effective", mass-produced, less labor-intensive coffees.
- Brazilian beans, however, have a silver lining. They are popular for ensuring "crema", the prized crown adorning a cup of Espresso, without the overwhelming presence of the intense robustas.

Bland and Brazil both start with a "B" for the same reason!
-Dave Olsen, senior vp, Starbucks Coffee

CARIBBEAN (See JAMAICAN)

CELEBES (See INDONESIA)

COLOMBIA (Coffee species: *Supremo, Excelso, Medellin Armenia, Manizales, Bogota, Bucaramanga*)
- The Colombian coffee industry, giant supplier for the "milds" category, is acknowledged worldwide as the "benchmark" in quality classic coffees.
- Colombia is the world's second-largest coffee producer, after Brazil.
- Most of the Colombian coffee is grown on the high altitudes of the Andes foothills, comprising hundreds of thousands of family farm enterprises, organized as federated co-operatives. Much pride and care is taken in the picking. The washing process after the harvest produces better beans.
- Colombian coffee is famous because of its successful marketing of Juan Valdez and his mule. Valdez represents and personalizes Colombian coffee.
- In general, Colombian coffee is clean, neutral arabicas, great for blending. It offers moderate acidity, body and a caramel-like sweetness.
- The most exported species in volume are the *Supremo* and *Excelso*, which are usually graded together for commercial coffee buyers. *Supremo* is the finest, larger prized beans fashioning a light body, sweet, aromatic and delicate flavor. It has slightly nutty undertones. The *Excelso* coffee species is inconsistently soft and slightly acidic.
- *Medellin, Armenia and Manizales*, marketed as MAM, are the principal species produced in central Colombia: acidic, rich and flavorful.

- Eastern Colombia produces the famous *Bogota*: rich, flavorful, not as acidic, and *Bucaramanga*: fine coffee with a rich flavor, low acidity and heavy body.

Colombian coffee is at its best a classic coffee;
for a coffee lover who wants a Rolls Royce, but can only afford a BMW!
-Kenneth Davids, Coffee (1981)

COSTA RICA (Coffee species: *Tarrazu, Tres Rios, Santa Rosa, Montbello, Juan Vinas and Alajuela*)

- The high altitude of Costa Rica coffee plantations determines the flavor of its coffees. These coffees are among the finest richest coffees in the world: robust richness of fragrance, exceptionally full body, fine mild flavor, sharply acidic.
- Interestingly enough, the acidic level of the beans increases with altitude. Costa Rican coffees are regarded as: "strictly hard beans", indicating that they were grown above 3,900 feet (1,189 metres) and "good hard bean", below 3,900 feet (1,189 metres).
- A good Costa Rican coffee is synonymous with a good Burgundy wine — rich and hearty; it exhibits the purest of flavors. The coffee from this region has a legendary classic completeness and balance — having everything and lacking nothing.
- The San Jose central plateau of Costa Rica is famous for its soil, volcanic nitrogen-rich ash and dust, 15 feet (4.5 metres) deep.
- The four most famous coffees are known by their district: *Tarrazu, Tres Rios, Heredia and Alajuela*.

I would stare into the black darkness of my Costa Rican coffee cup,
expecting a horrible bitter taste, however, my senses were surprised with
a beautiful fresh rich flavor, not bitter at all.
-Margaret Brown, a friend visiting Costa Rica, describing her cup of coffee

CUBA

- The mountains in Cuba are not very high, therefore the coffee from this region is not as acidic.
- The main exports of Cuban coffee are to Russian, Eastern Europe and France.

DOMINICAN REPUBLIC (Coffee species: *Santo Domingo, Barahona, Bani and Ocoa*)

- On the Dominican Republic east-axis of the mountain range border of the island, the best washed arabica coffee comes from *Bani* and *Ocoa*. They are known for being soft and mellow.
- Most of the coffee coming from this region of the world is romantically called Santo Domingo, after the country's former name.
- The Barahona are acidy and quite similar to Jamaican high mountain species.
- The coffees from this region are generally mid-range, fair to good body, pleasant to taste and not overbearing in acidity.

ECUADOR

- South of Colombia, along the Andes mountains, Ecuador produces an outstanding bean.
- The coffee from Ecuador is thin to medium body with sharp acidity.

EL SALVADOR

- This tiny country grows practically nothing but coffee.

- The best grade of coffee from El Salvador is called "strictly high grown". Its characteristics are slightly sweet, full body and medium acidity. This coffee is quite popular in France.

ETHIOPIA (Coffee species: Harrar or Ethiopian Mocha, Jimma, Abyssinian, Sidamo or Yirgacheffe)

- On the mountain plateaus of this country, coffee originated more than a millennium ago and today the tribesmen in this region still harvest the wild coffee berries.
- Ethiopian coffees have a very distinctive flavor and aroma, inconsistent and like no other coffee. The majority of the coffee produced is still gathered from "wild" trees, carelessly picked and dry processed using primitive methods. Often the coffees sold here are the "Ethiopian Harrar" or "Ethiopian Mocha" and "Abyssinian" coffee.
- Sometimes the other names above are used to denote the various districts of Ethiopia where they were grown.
- Harrar (named after the old capital of Ethiopia) is a winey, spicy, fruity, strong coffee.
- Yirgacheffe coffee has an exotic flowery fragrance.
- Yemen Mocha is the traditional, most-favored coffee from this area.

GUATEMALA (Coffee species: Cobans, Antiguas, Atilans, Huehuetenango)

- Guatemala neighbors Costa Rica, with its adored coffees. The soil here is similar to Costa Rica, rich in nitrogen due to its volcanic nature.
- Outside the old capital of Guatemala City, the coffee-terraced landscapes are breathtaking. This region grows the highest grades in the world, "strictly hard bean", indicating the coffee was grown at altitudes of 4,500 feet (1,372 metres) or higher, producing full-bodied, very acidy coffees with a soft mild, delightful flavor.
- The most famous are the Coban, Antigua and Atilans coffees.
- The Huehuetenango exhibits a powerful acidity and a bitter orange fruity flavor bouquet.
- A Guatemalan Antiguan coffee is replete with a perfect balance of body, acidity, sweet and smoky tones.

HAITI

- Haiti offers the best high-grown coffee. It resembles the famous Blue Mountain coffee from its neighboring country, Jamaica, with its sweet, mellow, rich, heavy-bodied characteristics.
- Haiti experiences heavy rainfall and has deep volcanic soil, accounting for the mellow sweetness of its coffee signature.
- Unfortunately, the Haitian government has enforced many prohibitions. A lack of enterprise has also resulted in low production from this region.

HAWAII (Coffee species: Kona)

- Hawaii is the only area in the United States which grows coffee – Kona coffee.
- Kona coffee is carefully cultivated on volcanic slopes, producing prized lustrous beans. It is also carefully processed.
- The coffee-growing industry in Hawaii is very small, and the labor costs are high. The entire coffee-growing area is two miles wide by twenty-five miles long (3.2 x 40 kilometers).
- Hawaii keeps the best of its coffee for itself, selling locally and to tourists for a higher profit margin.
- Hawaii's coffee stands for prestigious preservation, since its production is limited, and it should be appreciated. Kona coffee is medium-bodied, deliciously rich, and exudes an overwhelming aroma.

INDIA *(Coffee species: Mysore, Baba Budan, Niligris, and Sheverays, Coorg, Monsooned Malabar)*
- The state of Mysore, in southern India, has been producing arabica coffee since the mid-1600s when a muslim pilgrim, Baba Budan, brought back Yemen coffee beans to Mecca.
- Coffee supplied from this region is lower-priced, yet more consistent, than the better-known Indonesian coffees.
- The distinctive flavor of the Monsooned Malabar beans is one of the best; heavy body, a deep rich color, spice and little acidity.
- Their processing methods are called "monsooning", whereby unwashed arabica beans are stored in warehouses during their rainy season, then exposed to the hot air of the monsoon winds, drying them out for about a month. This treatment gives the beans from India a lightly spiced but mellow quality.
- Coffee auctions are usually held to sell the beans, often lumping the beans from various regions together.

INDONESIA AND NEW GUINEA *(Coffee species: Java, Sumatra Celebes, Mandheling, Ankola)*
- The gigantic islands of the Malay Archipelago, Java, Sumatra and Celebes in Indonesia, and Papua New Guinea grow the most famous coffees of the world.
- The coffees of Indonesia and New Guinea are noted for their richness, full body and a pronounced acidity which is gentle and deep.
- Java, which is synonymous with coffee itself, produces a mature, spicy, full-bodied strong coffee which is sometimes referred to as "strong-flavored".
- Sumatra coffees are some of the most popular in the specialty coffee trade, popular for their unusually strong, heavy body, and unique musty flavor. Of Sumatra's coffee growing regions, the Mandheling and Ankola coffees are the finest, with a syrupy richness, exquisite aroma, vibrant and flavorful.
- Celebes is similar to Sumatran coffee but possibly lighter and a little less rich, with a bit more acidity. Sometimes Celebes is referred to as Kalossi, another world-famous coffee, since Kalossi is the coffee capital of this island.

JAVA *(See INDONESIA)*

JAMAICA *(Coffee species: Jamaican Blue Mountain, High Mountain)*
- The most famous Caribbean coffee is, of course, the Jamaican Blue Mountain coffee.
- A true Blue Mountain should be absolutely exquisite, rich in flavor and aroma, full body and moderate acidity, a perfectly balanced beverage.
- Jamaican coffee is one of extremes, since the lowlands of Jamaica produce ordinary cheap filler blends, whereas the coffees grown on the Jamaican highlands rank as some of the world's best. For example, the Jamaican Blue Mountain, from the Wallensford Estates, is often called the "caviar of coffees". It is the world's most expensive and celebrated coffee.
- The High Mountain is a common boring coffee, with few attributes of the fine Blue Mountain coffee which is very scarce and hard to find.

KENYA *(Coffee species: Nairobi)*
- Kenyan coffee beans are grown on exceedingly high, 5,000 foot (1,524 metres) plateaus in the foothills of Mount Kenya.
- The high-quality processing methods are of a sophistication similar to the methods used in Costa Rica and Colombia because of the government's support to its coffee industry. With only ripe cherries being picked, and high-quality standards, these washed Kenyan arabica beans provide wondrous flavor, delightful full body and superior sparkling acidic coffee.

KONA (See HAWAII)

MEXICO (Coffee species: *Chiapas, Oaxaca Pluma, Coatepec, Huatusco, Orizaba*)
- Southern Mexico produces the finest Mexican coffees.
- The best coffee beans grown in Mexico are the fine estate-grown coffees of Veracruz, High Coatepec. The best, well-washed, most flavorful coffees are the Chiapas and Oaxaca Pluma, the growing region near the Guatemalan border where the beans are washed and dry processed.
- The Orizaba and Huatusco region beans rank close behind. The coffee brew most Mexicans drink is made from dry-processed beans. They are usually dark-roasted and glazed with sugar, producing a sweet heavy brew.
- The coffees of Mexico are not among the world's greatest coffees, because they often lack richness in acidity and fullness in body. They are low-grown, soft beans which do not produce good dark coffees.
- At its best, Mexican coffee delivers a pleasantly dry, light acidity, brisk cup of coffee.

MOCHA (See YEMEN)

MYSORE (See INDIAN)

NEW GUINEA (See INDONESIA)

NICARAGUA (Coffee species: *Jinotegas, Matagalpa*)
- This Central American country, as well as El Salvador, has recently begun to privatize and renovate its coffee industry in order to participate in the world's specialty coffee market categories.
- The coffees here are generally irregular, being neutral in flavor, fairly acidic and medium to light in body. Their middle-of-the-road characteristics make them ideal beans for blending.

PANAMA
- The washed arabica coffee beans produced in this region are quite competitive to the coffee product coming from Costa Rica.
- The quality is fine, with a full body, mild pleasant flavor and good acidity.

PERU (Coffee species: *Chanchamayo*)
- The Chanchamayo valley, in the high Andes mountain ranges, produces the Peruvian coffees which have the best reputation.
- They are generally a classic coffee, delicately acidic, thin to full body but flavorful.
- Unfortunately, exporters have damaged the reputation of Peruvian coffees since they mix the good beans with the average ones, delivering irregular, inconsistent-quality shipments.
- Production is low due to political and revolutionary upheavals.

SUMATRA (See INDONESIA)

TANZANIA (Coffee species: *Kilimanjaro, Mkibo Chagga*)

- Most of the Tanzanian arabicas are grown on the slopes of Mount Kilimanjaro, near the Kenyan border.
- Many of the coffees are still cultivated by tribes in the forest clearings on the mountain slopes.
- Smaller amounts are grown further south of this region. All of the Tanzanian coffees are exotic and characteristically sharp in nature. They tend to be full-bodied and fairly rich in flavor, tending toward a winey acidity.

UGANDA (Coffee species: *Bugishu*)

- The only high-grown quality arabica grown in this African region is the *Bugishu* beans. These beans are grown on the western slopes of Mount Elgon, on the Kenyan border, and produce a light-bodied typically winey acidity.
- African coffee beans are similar to Kenyan beans.
- The remaining Ugandan coffee beans are robustas, which are used mainly in instant coffees and as cheap fillers in blends.

VENEZUELA (Coffee species: *Caracas, Maracaibo coffees: Merida, Cucuta, Trujillo and Tachira*)

- The best of the Venezuelan coffees come from the western corner of the country, closer to Colombia. They are called *Maracaibos* beans (named after their outbound shipping port), and include *Cucuta* coffee.
- Of all the *Maracaibo* coffees, the *Merida* is the most distinctive. It offers a delicate flavor with an enticing aroma and hints of richness.
- The *Caracas* has a lighter body and attractive flavor which is quite popular in Spain and France.
- The various qualities of Venezuelan coffees depend greatly on the individual plantations.

YEMEN (Coffee species: *Mocha, Arabian*)

- The coffee we know as *Mocha* is grown on the mountains of Yemen, at the southwestern tip of the Arabian peninsula, opening up to the Red Sea.
- Mocha has become a nickname for coffee. It is known for its chocolately aftertaste, which has inspired the name "mocha" for the traditional mixture of hot chocolate and coffee.
- The beans here are harvested and processed as they have been for centuries, with dry-processed primitive methods. Although many of the beans from Yemen do not have standardized names, the Mattari and Sanani Mocha coffee beans, from two of Yemen's four regions, are the most common of the true Mochas which are exported around the world.

ZAIRE (See ZIMBABWE)

ZIMBABWE (Zaire)

- The washed arabicas of these African coffee regions are grown in the Ruwenzori Mountains, in the Kivu and Ituri regions. Political unrest rules the coffee harvests, producing uncertain qualities and availability from year to year.
- The coffees from this region have a pleasant flavor but are very high in acidity. This makes the African arabicas ideal for complementing other coffee blends.
- Unfortunately, the good years depend on the harvest, and political stability and climate variables; therefore, this region can rarely offer consistency in its coffee industry.

Making coffee in the French press versus the flip-drip method,
is like French kissing instead of a kiss on the cheek!

-ANONYMOUS

PART 3
COFFEE MACHINES 'N' METHODS/
BREWING TECHNIQUES 'N' TIPS

There are many ways of preparing a good cup of coffee. You'd be hard-pressed (or perhaps French pressed!) to finding a bad "cup of joe" these days. From the sexy French press, to the finicky flip-drip coffeepot, all methods have one thing in common. They are all based on using hot water to extract the flavors and aromas from the ground coffee beans.

Personal taste dictates the strength or weakness of the coffee, as well as the method with which to make it. Various methods offer different advantages and disadvantages. Each method achieves a distinguished coffee character, and attracts different audiences for reasons of culture, habit, taste and/or lifestyle.

Therefore, the method of choice is based on personal preference and priority; whether that is quality, convenience, simplicity, theatrics or, perhaps, just plain passion.

Here we go! Different brews for different crews!

The following pages will outline the principal coffee brewing methods:
• the filter drip methods (automatic or manual versions)
• the French press or pot plunger (Bodum) method
• the vacuum pot
• the Middle Eastern method (Turkish/Greek)
• the percolator method (boiling coffee)

A dedicated section, *Espresso Machines 'n' Methods/Brewing Techniques 'n' Tips*, follows at the end of this chapter for:
• the Moka-style Stovetop method(s)
• the Neapolitan Flip-Drip method
• the pump, piston and electric steam-powered Espresso machine

Please keep in mind, however, that besides the brewing method used, the finished coffee/Espresso beverage will also differentiate greatly, based on the following factors:
• the choice of roasted coffee bean used (see page 25)
• the correct amount and fineness of the coffee grind (see page 31)

The cone-shaped bag . . . unfailingly clear, fragrant and seductive.

-Claudia Roden, Coffee – a Connoisseur's Companion

FILTER DRIP METHODS (automatic and manual)

These drip methods are the most widely used in North America and northern Europe. They permit the use of very fine coffee grinds for quick and thorough coffee extraction. Initially, a cone-shaped paper filter is placed into a plastic, glass or ceramic cone-shaped holder. This filter holder sits on top of a flameproof glass carafe or coffeepot. Fine-ground coffee is then placed into the filter. Boiling water is poured onto the fresh ground coffee. Fresh brewed coffee then "drips" into a coffeepot or carafe, either automatically or manually.

AUTOMATIC "set 'em and forget 'em" DRIP METHOD

The Method:

In an electric drip coffee maker, fine to medium-ground coffee is placed into a cone-shaped paper filter. Hot water is automatically heated and drips through the coffee bed, trickling into a pot that sits on the machine's warming plate, literally called "the burner".

Advantages:

- "Set 'em and forget 'em!" Ideal anytime, for a quick, convenient, automatic cup of coffee – especially first thing in the morning!
- Beans down, it is the best way to make coffee for a crowd.
- Easy cleanup – the paper filters can be disposed of easily.
- A reusable wire mesh filter may be used as an environmentally friendly alternative to disposable paper filters.

Disadvantages:

- Bleached or natural paper filters are most commonly used to filter the coffee grounds, however, paper filters absorb some of the coffee's flavor.
- A burnt, slightly bitter taste results when the pot of coffee remains on the machine's burner too long (20 minutes or longer), overheating it, and throwing the finished flavor of the coffee out of balance. To remedy this "burner" flavor in the coffee, transfer the finished fresh brew immediately to an insulated thermal carafe. (Be sure to first preheat the carafe with hot water, so the cold glass lining inside the carafe does not cool down the fresh hot coffee.)

Recommended Coffee Grind: Medium grind for paper filters. Fine to medium grind for metal filters.

Brewing Tips:

- To prevent a burnt flavor, never keep the coffee pot on "the burner" longer than 20 minutes.
- Keep the coffee warm, if necessary, in a thermal carafe.
- Blend the aromas of the finished coffee by swirling the coffee in the pot just prior to pouring the first cup of coffee.

MANUAL DRIP (MELITTA) METHOD

The Method:

Water is heated to boiling in a kettle. Once the boiled water is allowed to rest for 10 to 15 seconds, it is then poured manually onto fresh fine to medium coffee grounds, which have been placed into a paper or wire mesh filter, designed to sit in a wedge-shaped filter holder. The coffee then drips into a container of choice, either a glass carafe, thermal carafe or single mug.

Advantages:
- Portion and waste control are benefits of this method, if only one to three cups are required.
- Complete control of coffee-to-water ratio and water temperature ensures a better-quality coffee than the automatic drip method.
- The coffee flavors are not burnt or destroyed, as in the automatic method, where the coffee carafe is left sitting on a burner.
- This method is portable – great for camping!

Disadvantages:
- More time and attention is required for this method (however, a better quality of coffee is guaranteed), since one must boil water separately, then manually pour the water through the coffee in the filter.

Recommended Coffee Grind: Use medium grind for paper filters; fine to medium for metal filters.

Brewing Tips:
- Be sure to heat the container gently by rinsing it with hot water before filtering coffee into it.
- Once the water has boiled, allow it to rest 10 to 15 seconds before pouring it onto coffee grounds in the cone-shaped filter.
- Premoisten the coffee grounds by initially pouring hot water over the dry grounds, wetting them evenly. (Premoisten example – if 1/2 cup (125 mL) of ground coffee is used, "wet" them with 1/2 cup (125 mL) of hot water. Wait 30 seconds before pouring the rest of the water through in this case, the remaining 2 1/2 cups (625 mL). This initial contact of water with the coffee grounds releases a concentration of delicate coffee aromas and flavors. The "wet" grounds create a smaller, denser volume, packed into the deep bed, for the hot water to flow evenly through.

FRENCH PRESS or PLUNGER POT METHOD (the "Bodum" pot)

This simple easy method produces an extremely rich, robust coffee. It is beans down the next best brew to Espresso. Medium to coarse coffee grounds directly "infuse" with slightly cooled boiling water, creating a promising marriage of flavor and aroma.

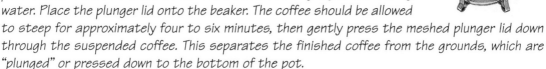

The Method:

Prewarm the glass beaker by rinsing it with hot water. Place the preferred amount of coffee into the beaker and add slightly cooled boiling water. Place the plunger lid onto the beaker. The coffee should be allowed to steep for approximately four to six minutes, then gently press the meshed plunger lid down through the suspended coffee. This separates the finished coffee from the grounds, which are "plunged" or pressed down to the bottom of the pot.

*Advantages: ***

- This method guarantees the richest body of coffee (if done properly), except for Espresso.
- The steeping time is less. Pressure application is slight; the water is hotter; the ratio of coffee to water is higher.
- The coffee grounds steep in water just under the boiling point, with no further boiling or burning preserving the dark, delightful coffee aroma and flavor without a trace of bitterness.
- The delicate aroma of the coffee oils are NOT removed by a paper filter.
- This method is quick and it is also portable.

Disadvantages:

- The coffee may be cooled down by the time it has finished steeping. (See tips for remedy).
- If the coffee grind is too fine, there may be difficulty in pressing down the plunger lid because of increased surface tension.
- Fine coffee sediment will remain at the bottom of the cup if medium to coarse grind is not used.
- Extra clean up is required.

Recommended Coffee Grind: Medium to coarse grind.

Brewing Tips:

- Measure two level tablespoons (30 mL) of ground coffee for every six ounces (170 mL) of water.
- Water selection is also key. The higher quality of water used, the better your coffee will taste.
- Rinse the glass plunger pot first with "hot" water; add the "slightly cooled" (approximately 212°F or 100°C) boiled water to the coffee grounds, then wrap a terry cloth towel around the pot during steeping. This will keep the finished coffee hot longer.

* BONUS ADVANTAGE: THE PLUNGER POT CAN DOUBLE AS A MILK FROTHER/FOAMER TO MAKE FROTHY CAPPUCCINOS AND LATTES!

HEAT a cup of milk (non-fat milk works best), soy or rice milk in a saucepan on the stove, or in a microwave. DO NO OVERHEAT OR SCALD THE MILK. (It should be heated just until it is too hot to put your finger into it).
POUR the milk into a clean, rinsed plunger pot.
PUMP the plunger (top part) up and down in the pot for several minutes, like a butter churn. The milk will expand in volume by three to four times, creating froth for cappuccinos and lattes.

VACUUM POT METHOD (Silex, Cona or glass balloon)

This is the most unique and dramatic way of preparing an excellent, full-flavored cup of coffee. Two glass globes, one set into another, with a filter, suspend over a heat source. The set-up looks more like a magical kerosene lamp than a coffee pot! It's sophisticated and attractive appeal was fashionable around the First World War and then again during the sixties and seventies, however, it has lost much of its popularity, mainly due to the finicky and peculiar method.

The Method:

Place the filter into the upper funnel and place the coarsely ground coffee in the top glass globe. The coffee sits loosely around the filter, and the top is open. Set the lower globe on the stand and fill the bottom glass with boiling water from a kettle (if you wait for the heat source or flame to boil the water it will take hours!). Fit the upper globe tightly, creating an airtight seal with the lower globe, and set the pot over the low flame. Steam pressure will force the heated water up through the tube into the upper globe, where the heated water begins to stir the ground coffee. Allow the coffee to steep, then turn off the flame. As the lower globe cools and contracts, a "vacuum" forms, sucking the coffee down into the lower globe. When all the coffee has filtered down, remove the upper globe and pour the coffee! Your guests will be impressed by your chemistry talents!

Advantages:
- Portable, can be taken anywhere without worry about electrical outlets.
- If you enjoy the theatrics in making an exotic brew, this method is impressive and entertaining.
- This method delivers an excellent, pure, fine coffee using a classic pot with cloth filters.

Disadvantages:
- Very time consuming. You definitely have to "go with the flow" with this one, since "steam pressure" is the driving force.
- The coffee brewing process must be totally complete before the top globe is removed. Patience and timing are crucial because, if the top is removed too soon, coffee will be spilled all over.
- Plastic models produce a muddy-looking brown coffee.
- This is a finicky and complex device.

Recommended Coffee Grind: Medium to fine grind.

Brewing Tips:
- To help speed up this method, boil water separately in a kettle, then pour it into the lower globe and place it over the heat source to begin the steam pressure process.
- Make certain the entire brewing process is complete before removing top globe.

MIDDLE EASTERN METHOD (Turkish, Greek)

Various Mideastern countries have their own variations of this method, such as Turkish or Greek, however, all the variations are similar in that the coffee grounds are boiled with water and may also be brewed with sugar. This method produces a very heavy-bodied, somewhat syrupy brew.

The Method:
- A coffee pot called an "ibrik" (Arabian) or "briki" (Greek) is used. This is a long-handled copper or brass coffee pot.
- For two servings: place two heaping teaspoons (14 mL) of pulverized powdered coffee grounds into the pot along with ½ cup (125 mL) water and two heaping teaspoons (14 mL) of sugar.
- Bring to a boil.
- Remove the ibrik or briki from the heat source; let the froth subside; stir.
- This heating process is repeated twice to produce a thick "black, muddy" brew.
- The coffee is then poured into small two-ounce (60mL) cups, and the grounds are allowed to settle before the coffee is consumed.

Advantages:
- Once the grounds have settled, this heavy coffee is surprisingly mild and sweet, if enough sugar has been added to it!
- The brewing process may be impressive and entertaining for guests.

Disadvantages:
- Producing the thin head of brown foam on the surface of the coffee is authentic to Mideastern coffee methods, however, it is not always achieved by a novice. Practice, practice!

Recommended Coffee Grind: Pulverized powdered fine grind (as fine as cake flour!).

Brewing Tips:
- Never fill the ibrik to more than half its capacity. The coffee "puffs" up (foams) and the pot must accommodate this expansion. Otherwise it will spill over.
- When the coffee "puffs" up, and is about to boil over, remove it from the stove and pour a bit of the ceremonial foam into the serving cups. The usual sugar dose in the Middle East is equal parts sugar and ground coffee, however, this can be increased or decreased to suit personal taste preferences.
- Bring the coffee to just a simmering boil, do not overboil. Serve immediately once this has been repeated two to three times.
- For spiced variations, add cardamom seeds, cinnamon, nutmeg or cloves to the pot while the coffee is boiling.

PERCOLATOR METHOD (boiling coffee)

Boiled coffee is spoiled coffee! This less-preferred method of brewing coffee was quite popular during the 1930s and 1940s. Boiling water is force-pumped up through a tube, mixing with a basket of dry coffee grounds. This method actually "boils" the coffee, driving away the delicate coffee aromatics and producing an over-extracted, bitter brew.

The Method:
- Water is poured into a pot.
- Medium to coarse-ground coffee is placed in the filter basket, inserted into the percolator, covered and either placed on stove burner or, if electric, plugged in.
- The heated water creates a steam pressure and it is forced up through the coffee basket. It repeatedly circulates over the bed of coffee grounds.
- As the coffee brews, it is repeatedly boiled to create steam to force it back up again through the coffee basket, approximately six to eight times.

Advantages:
- None

Disadvantages:
- The delicate coffee aromatics and oils are burned off, and the coffee achieved with this method is offensively overextracted. Perked coffee is harsh and bitter.
- This overkill "boiled", perked coffee has negative health benefits attached to it. (Please refer to the "cholesterol" issue in the Coffee and Your Health chapter, page 192.)

Recommended Coffee Grind: Medium to coarse grind.

Boiled coffee is spoiled coffee, so,
thou shalt not percolate thy coffee!
-ANONYMOUS

Perfection has one grave fault it is apt to be dull.

-W. Somerset Maugham (1874-1965)

TIPS FOR MAKING THE PERFECT CUP OF COFFEE

Perfection is purely a personal choice. No matter how much better a person thinks the coffee is, your own palate is certainly "the best judge of the better java." Whether you are taking the coffee straight up or immersed in a lofty lather of frothed milk, there are certain freshness fundamentals which will "awaken" your coffee and make it live up to its aromatic and flavorsome potential. Every ingredient should be the best, the freshest, and every technique should be performed properly to ensure a perfect coffee beverage. Of course, the best coffee teacher is practice, practice, practice!

CLEAN EQUIPMENT:
- *Baking soda and warm water is a great cleaning agent for filters, coffeemakers, etc. If sediments remain after usage, odors can be absorbed, and the remaining coffee oils can turn rancid.*

CLEAN WATER:
- *Never use tap water, because of the dissolved base minerals in the hard water.*
- *Chlorine-free, filtered water, or distilled, is most preferable (even Brita water is ideal). Another reason for filtered water is that the mineral salts, which can interfere with the extraction of the coffee, have been removed.*
- *Cold water is better because it hasn't been sitting in the pipes or the boiler for a long time.*
- *Softened water is a personal choice. Some people do not mind it; others say the phosphates and agents in the soft water produce a soapy-tasting coffee.*

PROPER GRIND AND BREWING TIME:
- *The correct grind and length of brewing (contact) time the coffee requires varies according to the brewing method. (See page 30.)*

PROPER QUANTITY:
- *A standard rule for a cup of coffee, using a fine coffee grind, is 1 tablespoon (15 mL) per 1 cup/8 ounces (250 mL) of water. If a double strength is preferred, use one rounded tablespoon (22 mL) to 1/2 cup/4 ounces (125 mL) of water. If using a coarser grind, as much as 4 rounded tablespoons (88 mL) to 2 1/2 cups (625 mL) of water may be used.*
- *The most important rule here is: follow your own taste. This is a very personal choice.*

PROPER TEMPERATURE:
- *The correct water temperature is somewhere between 195 to 205°F (90 to 96°C) when the water is in contact with the coffee grounds, and 185 to 190°F (85 to 88°C) when the finished coffee is in the cup.*
- *A good reference is the wattage on the coffee or Espresso maker. The higher the watts, the more powerful the heater, and the better the coffee should be. A preferred machine rates over 1,000 watts, however, most home machines range around 850 watts.*

Espresso is the dark karmic soul of coffee . . .
prepared with passion . . . not the same old grind!

-SUSAN M. ZIMMER

PART 4
ESPRESSO MACHINES 'N' METHODS/BREWING TECHNIQUES 'N' TIPS

Espresso coffee brewing methods are in a class of their own. Espresso is an "extreme coffee", famous for its intense flavor, signature aroma and amazing brewing methods. Whether Espresso coffee is consumed as an unadorned straight "shot"; all dressed up with satiny foamed milk; or added to our much-loved mochaccinos; specific factors differentiate this process from regular coffee brewing methods.

The creative difference of the Espresso method is the prevailing high "pressure" being applied to the "hot", not "boiling" water. The water is then forced through the finely ground coffee at a fast speed. The ideal pressure for making an Espresso is 9 bars of atmospheric pressure (125-140 pounds/57-64 kg).

High-tech, high-cost commercial Espresso machines are capable of creating this pressurized extraction to produce an Espresso in its finest form. These monster machines usually achieve the aroma, body and crema characteristics of a true Espresso.

How does one reproduce this dark, delightful Espresso at home?

Making Espresso coffee doesn't have to become a grind! Today's technology offers Espresso makers in a wide range of prices, working in different ways and achieving various results. Low-tech and high-tech methods are offered; costing low-tech and high-tech dollars! All of them exhibit the same pressure principles, however, they all work by different processes.

For serious Espresso lovers, willing to pay serious dollars, the high-tech, high-cost systems are:
• the pump machine
• the piston-driven machine
• the electric steam-powered machine

All of these machines come in expensive home and commercial versions. If your passionate palate is intrigued with technology, and your budget can afford it, then the sophisticated Espresso equipment may be for you. Taking all of this one level higher, the Espresso connoisseur can purchase a "supersonic, automatic mother-of-a-machine", with a price tag of over $1,000 attached to it.

Before you take out a second mortgage on your house, or a bank loan, let's consider some low-tech, simplified solutions. These methods, which may require a budget of about $20 to $30 dollars are:
• the moka-style stovetop method(s)
• the Neapolitan flip-drip method

These less-sophisticated, but more-economical methods are reliable and ideal for milk-based specialty coffee beverages. The home-brewed Espresso may not win first prize in a professional barista contest, but Italians and other Europeans have perfected these humble apparatus methods over many decades. They are the next best thing to a "perfect" Espresso. For instance, the moka-style stovetop is perhaps the most popular Espresso apparatus. It is found in every Italian household.

The "stovetop pot version, brewing the Espresso directly into the cup" method, (the method is simpler than the name!) is sworn to be ideal by some executive chefs with whom I am personally acquainted. Unfortunately, the glorious crema, which crowns a perfect Espresso, is sometimes sadly missed on the home front. This is because most home Espresso machines cannot obtain the required intense pressure of 9 ATM, necessary to extract an emulsion of oils and colloids from the coffee grind. If you are lucky, and crema does crown your home brew, count it an an astral blessing!

The following at-a-glance overview of making Espresso outlines various methods, pros/cons, old Italian secrets and simple, reliable tips. The simple more economical methods are featured first, with the high-cost, high-tech methods to follow. Hopefully this review will broaden awareness of the various methods available for brewing Espresso coffee, and cultivate another reason for drinking it — for the ceremonial ritual in creating it and the sheer satisfaction of savoring it.

I set my timer for 3 minutes. Very methodical . . . nothing must interfere with this coffee technique.
-RAYMOND CHANDLER, THE LONG GOOD-BYE

MOKA-STYLE (non-electric) STOVETOP ESPRESSO METHOD

This simple steel apparatus is a traditional home model. It brews Espresso coffee on the top of a stove. In its world-famous hourglass shape, the moka brewer is available in stainless steel and ceramic. Aluminum is not recommended. The moka stovetop brewer uses the pressure, which results from boiling the water to brew the coffee. This method of making Espresso produces approximately 1^1/2 to 3 bars of pressure, not the ideal 9 bars of pressure, however, enough to deliver some extra texture, body, and the emulsion which gives Espresso coffee more flavor and richness.

Nonetheless, many of the "seasoned" Italian Espresso connoisseurs prefer this method to any of the high-tech furnace-like contraptions today's technology offers. All of these Italians can't be wrong!

The Method:

The moka pot has two chambers, with a filter between them. Cold water is placed in the bottom chamber to the level of the safety valve and finely ground coffee is placed "loosely" into the filter, which is then placed in the bottom pot. Screw the upper chamber onto the bottom. The pot is placed over medium-high heat. The water heats up and the resulting trapped pressure is forced up through the coffee grounds. In about three minutes the coffee will begin to trickle into the top chamber of the pot and begin to gurgle and emerge out of the spout. The heat is turned off, or the pot is removed from the heat source and allowed to rest for a few minutes. The Espresso coffee is finished when the top chamber is full and just steam comes out of the spout.

Other Designs:

"The stovetop pot which brews the Espresso coffee directly into the cup," the convenience speaks for itself, it also prewarms the cup at the same time! It works similarly to the moka-style pot, however, it also enables you to brew only one or two cups at a time, rather than an entire pot. This pot is the pot used by The Banff Centre's executive Chef Hegnauer. Using a $20 stovetop pot which brews Espresso coffee directly into the cup, you can make an excellent double Espresso and couple it with satiny foamed milk. You can whisk in a separate saucepan to produce a to-die-for cappuccino, see page 66.

Advantages:

* Perfect for caffe lattes and acceptable for cappuccinos!
* Although this method does not guarantee a "perfect" Espresso, it certainly is capable of producing a reliable, rich, home-brewed Espresso coffee which, when coupled with a separate milk foamer device, see French press milk-foaming tips on page 45, offers a thrifty alternative for making cappuccinos, lattes and mochaccinos.
* A simple, reliable way to make home-style Espresso coffee. It is economical and low-maintenance.
* Very space-efficient, convenient, consistent and easy to keep clean.

Disadvantages:

* It is difficult to brew one cup at at time.
* Aluminum is not recommended since the metal interacts with the coffee, giving an off-taste.

Recommended Coffee Grind: Fine to medium grind.

Brewing Tips:

(These tips are from Janice DiMillo, my lifelong Italian-Polish friend, who lives in the heart of Little Italy, Toronto, Ontario, Canada.)

* Aluminum moka pots are not recommended since the metal interacts with the coffee acids to produce a flavor which will be off balance.
* Use coffee which is specifically roasted and ground for Espresso making. Ordinary drip coffee blends will not work.
* Experiment with different brands to find one to suit your taste, since different brands can change the flavor, aroma and body of the finished Espresso coffee.
* Do not compact or tamp down the coffee grounds when placing them into the filter. Instead, "mound" the coffee high in the filter before screwing both chambers together.
* Before screwing on the top chamber, wipe off the rim of the bottom chamber to ensure a tight seal.
* Make certain that the heat source is not on high, but rather on medium or just below medium because once the water begins to boil, the Espresso brewing process is rapid, and the coffee can become over-extracted and bitter.
* As soon as coffee begins to emerge from the spout, remove the pot from the heat and let the rest slowly brew through. You may leave the top open so you can see when the coffee starts to come up to the top chamber. When the coffee flow begins to sputter foam, turn off the heat and allow the rest to brew through. The Espresso coffee is ready when only steam comes out of the spout.

NEAPOLITAN FLIP-DRIP BREWER

Italians call this method "Neapolitan", the French call it "café filtre", and Americans may refer to it as "macchinetta". This method is a bit theatrical in that it requires a manual flipping of the coffee pot brewer, thus the name – flip-drip!

The Method:

The flip-drip has two separate cylinder pots, which are attached, one on top of the other, at the waist of the pot. The bottom pot has a spout. Cold water is placed in the bottom "spouted" pot, and finely-ground coffee is secured in the two-sided filter chamber in the "waist" of the pot. The top pot is then fitted or latched on. The pot is placed on the stove over high heat. When the water boils, and steam comes out of the spout, the pot is removed from the heat and flipped over. *Flip it to drip it!* The hot water drips through the coffee into the empty side of the pot. Voila, fresh coffee.

Advantages:
* The flip-drip method is fun, easy and economical.
* The Italian metal flip pot produces a rich strong coffee, since the coffee (3 scoops) to water (1½ cups) ratio is higher than usual.

Disadvantages:
* Sediment usually collects at the bottom of the coffee cup. (See coffee grinding guide on page 31).
* If handles are not heatproof, the flipping is not fun!
* Aluminum or iron pots are not recommended since the metal interacts with the coffee and produces a burnt aftertaste. (Silver or copper-lined stainless steel are recommended).
* Coffee should be transferred to a thermal carafe if it is to be kept warm for awhile.

Recommended Coffee Grind: Medium to coarse for Italian flip-drip pots; medium to fine for the American-made flip pots.

Brewing Tips:
* Preheat the bottom half of the pot with hot water before brewing.
* Let the boiling water rest from ten to fifteen seconds before flipping the pot.
* Do not overfill the two-sided filter chamber with coffee grounds.

HIGH-TECH (HIGH COST) ESPRESSO MACHINES

This section covers the machines that can be costly and confusing, predictable or problematic, flashy and foolproof! However, practice does make perfect – Espresso!

If operated carefully, these sophisticated home Espresso systems can come close to delivering a professional cup, like those from your corner cafe! The fundamental difference with these machines is the increased pressure which is applied to the hot, not boiling, water to produce the special extraction necessary to create the emulsion of coffee particles, oils and colloids from the ground coffee.

Another difference is that the hot water and ground coffee does not stay in contact too long. The extraction is extremely quick. Almost instantly , as the pressurized water saturates every grain of ground coffee, the golden Espresso nectar begins to trickle into the cup. The undesirable chemicals in the coffee do not get extracted. The desirables, however, the aromas and pleasant flavors, remain in the finished brew.

With the coffee being ground seconds before it is brewed, every cup is fresh.

If your discriminating palate has bought into the theatrical mechanics of a more elaborate Espresso machine, then the following, at-a-glance profile of three basic systems may offer helpful information and tips. If you are searching for a method which best suits your needs and lifestyle, then reviewing this profile may help you choose.

Rather than elaborating on the methods in each machine category, I recommend that you read and follow the instruction manual for the individual machine you have, or are choosing, since each machine has different features and manufacturers offer different directions. The at-a-glance profile does however spotlight the pros and cons of each type of machine, recommends the suitable coffee grind, and provides brewing tips.

PUMP ESPRESSO MACHINES

This expensive method of making Espresso coffee is comparable to a commercial machine. The operator pilots the control switch to activate the pump, which raises the heat in the boiler (or heating coil). This creates an intensified pressure to force the water through the coffee bed, producing a creamier quality Espresso coffee – usually crowned with crema! These machine models usually have a valve for frothing and heating milk for milk-based specialty coffees. The home machines use a vibration pump rather than the rotary pump of the commercial versions.

Advantages:
- This machine supplies the proper pressure to ensure a very good Espresso.
- Certain models have heavy solid metal filters, filter holders, group heads, and retain the heat better than some models with lightweight equipment.
- Models with a large capacity, refillable water reservoir can produce a continuous supply of pressure, to make many Espresso drinks without any interruption.
- Achieves a relatively rapid brewing temperature.

Disadvantages:
- This system is very noisy and is not space efficient.
- The higher-quality solid models are built like tanks; boilers are built of durable brass and are expensive, usually priced about $400 dollars.
- It is very sensitive to the coffee grind size being used.
- It's recommended to position the machine near a sink, since it is messy to use and requires extensive cleanup.

Recommended Coffee Grind: Fine (the grind has to be just right in order to produce the crema).

Grinding Tip: The ground coffee should feel like fine sand, with a bit of abrasiveness to it when you rub the coffee between your fingers. It should NOT feel as fine as cake flour.

Brewing Tips:
- If possible use water from a filter pitcher, or non-mineralized water. The worst enemy of these machines is the mineral deposits which are left by tap water. Also, your Espresso will taste better.
- Before brewing any Espresso, perform a "blind" brew by running water through the machine without any coffee. This heats up all the metal elements and prewarms the cups too! A preheated machine is also a step closer to obtaining crema on the Espresso.
- Prime the pump to freshen the water in the boiler. This will also flush out any air pockets.
- If only one cup is being made, throw out the first cup of brewed Espresso. The second cup will always taste better. (Maybe that's how "The Second Cup" coffee chain franchise's name was born!).

PISTON (LEVER) MACHINES

The piston machine is appropriately named since the spring-loaded or hand-operated (or shall we say "bicep-operated") piston is the main characteristic of the machine.

The piston does the job of the motor, the pump and the brewing switches – producing the same pressure as a pump machine. The piston is lifted, drawing water into the cylinder below the piston, above the coffee bed, then the operator presses it down, pressing the water through the coffee bed. Spring-loaded machines have a spring above the piston to exert pressure on the water as it goes through the coffee.

This functional antique was very popular to and during the sixties, until the push-button pump moved into the piston's territory. Today, they may be difficult to find, however, the piston machines are still regarded, by some professionals, as among the finest machines made since they allow for closer, hands-on (or arms-on!) control in making Espresso.

Advantages:
- Looks very romantic, impressive and makes for a great conversation piece.
- Produces a quality Espresso (if used properly!).
- Simple in structure and design.
- This system is not as noisy as the pump machine.
- There is more control of the brewing pressure in combination with the size of coffee grind.
- Low maintenance, reliable durable machines; fewer parts – fewer malfunctions.
- Once the water heats up (when it finally does!), the temperature is usually hotter, more ideal (around 190°F/188°C).

If you don't produce a quality Espresso, at least your biceps will have had a good workout!

Disadvantages:
- Very labor intensive. The pressure applied is directly linked to the strength in your arm!
- If the operator does not apply enough pressure to the lever, the Espresso will not be good.
- Conversely, if you press too hard, it will not be good either. Very inconsistent results.
- This machine is not space efficient.
- Time consuming – heating up the water reservoir for coffee-brewing (same reservoir for milk frothing) can take up to 15 minutes. The water reservoir in this machine cannot be refilled while in use. It must be allowed to cool down, refilled and then heated up again.
- Water reservoir capacity is limited since it functions for coffee-brewing and milk-frothing.

Recommended Coffee Grind: Fine grind.

Brewing Tips:
- Size of the coffee grounds is crucial to producing a quality Espresso. If the grind is too coarse, the lever will go down almost effortlessly, since there is no resistance in the coffee bed, and only dirty water will be delivered into the cup. If the grind is too fine, you may have to overexert your biceps to push the lever down. It will be extremely difficult since now there is too much resistance for the water to pass through the coffee bed.
- When the light indicates the machine is ready to brew, lift the lever almost immediately or it may be too difficult to push back down.

ELECTRIC (STEAM POWERED) MACHINES

Electric Espresso machines function like a "glorified" moka stovetop pot. The biggest difference between the two is the price and the heat source. This overstated machine costs about four to five times more than a simple moka stovetop Espresso pot, and is equipped with an electric heat source instead of the humble burner on the stove!

Sure there is the bonus of the milk-steaming nozzle; which can be as useless as the disconnected hose of a fire hydrant! The pressure generated from the small boiler has only enough pressure to push hot water through the coffee bed. Any leftover steam pressure is usually insufficient to foam the milk properly, if you are planning to make specialty coffees. Many of these are simple aerating devices, which force the air in the room, along with the steam, into the milk.

Unfortunately, the design of these machines is sleek and sexy, attracting consumers, only to disappoint them with inadequate pressure, performance and capabilities.

Advantages:
- A quick-fix method, this is a convenient way to make a lazy Espresso or a caffe latte.
- It is not sensitive to the grind of the coffee – anything goes with this machine!
- It is capable of making several cups at a time – making quantity but not quality!
- Heat is provided by a built-in electric element (no need to turn on the stove).
- The models which offer a switch to turn off the flow of coffee, allow for overextraction control in the brewing process.
- They also provide a means to divert the trapped pressure in the boiler to the next step of frothing the milk (if specialty coffees are being made).

Disadvantages:
- The electric Espresso machines fool people by their attractive designs; disappointing consumers by their incapability of supplying enough pressure to create a true Espresso. Most of the time they do not deliver any crema! If they do, count it as an astral crema blessing!
- It is an expensive alternative to the more economical moka stovetop method. Essentially, the Espresso results from the two are comparable.
- The equipment attachments: filter, filter holder and group head are usually flimsy and light-weight, which does not ensure a tight seal.
- Not space efficient.
- Generally, there is not enough pressure to steam a small pitcher of milk. Sometimes another purchase for a steamer gadget is necessary, or see tips on page 62.
- Complicated to clean up.

Recommended Coffee Grind: Medium to fine grind.

Brewing Tips:
- When using a model which offers an on/off switch to stop the flow of coffee, stop the brew cycle somewhere after the mid-point to prevent overextraction.

Espresso is pleasure . . . if it isn't perfect where is the pleasure?
-SUSAN M. ZIMMER

FOUR "M" MUSTS FOR MAKING PERFECT ESPRESSO

The Italians, who are Espresso experts, refer to some traditional rules which are key to producing the ultimate coffee experience: a perfect cup of Espresso. There are four Italian "M's" which are carried out conscientiously by the "barista", the Espresso bartender. Barista is an honorable employment title which is earned through proven skill and experience, fusing art and science.

Many of us may never achieve this professional status, however, the following four Italian guidelines may help us to create a more perfect Espresso.

LA MACCHINA (pronounced MA-KEEN-A): THE MACHINE
- The home-based barista may use a smaller version of the more expensive restaurant-style Espresso machine, however, the machine must be able to heat the water to 194°F (90°C) and also be able to exert a pressure of at least 9 ATM.
- The Espresso machine must be operating efficiently and it's utensils kept clean at all times.
- The economical stovetop moka Espresso maker will produce a strong Espresso coffee, however, it will usually lack the rich creamy intensity, due to the lack of pressure. (The stovetop method, however, does produce a perfect coffee for caffe lattes).

LA MICSELSA (pronounced MIS-SHAY-LA): THE COFFEE BLEND
- The coffee beans selected, roasted and blended should provide a harmonious balance between bitterness and acidity, producing a rich full body, with a fragrant aroma, as well as possessing a thick caramelly texture. Espresso coffee blends are usually 100 percent arabica, from various origins.
- Personally, I prefer a coffee bean blend of 80 percent arabica and 20 percent robusta. The arabica proportion provides rich, round smooth coffee body and the robusta proportion produces strength and intensity, responsible for the lingering almost nutty aftertaste.
- Ultimately, the coffee-blend which is chosen is a matter of personal taste.

IL MACHINDOSATORE (pronounced MA-CHEE-NA-TSEE-ONAY): THE GRINDING
- To achieve the freshest flavor from the coffee beans, one should always grind them just before use, since fine ground coffee left exposed loses its flavor very quickly. (Fine ground coffee increases the coffee's surface area, thereby allowing oxygen and light to steal the coffee's precious aromas!)
- A burr-type grinder is ideal since the coffee grind can be adjusted to suit each individual Espresso machine. The ideal extraction time (which is the length of time the hot water is in contact with the coffee grounds) for home-brewing methods, is 15 to 20 seconds.
- Since the brewing time for Espresso coffee is so short, the grind of the coffee should be fine and powdery, so that the hot water can steep through the even fine grounds at a consistent and uniform pace. The extraction rate should be quick and thorough.

LA MANO (pronounced MAH-NO): "THE HAND" MAKING THE ESPRESSO
- *The hand of the Espresso operator and his skill ensure that the previous three rules are followed!*
- *The hand is also responsible for dispensing the correct amount of coffee, known as the "dose". Ideally, a dose is 1/4 to 1/2 ounce/7 to 12 grams of coffee per 1 to 1 1/2 ounces/30 to 42 mL of clean water. This dose amount may vary, depending on the coffee grind size and blend.*
- *The hand performs "the tamping" (pressing down) of the coffee grounds in the portafilter of the machine. After tamping the grounds must be even and firm, to allow the water to filter through the coffee for a consistent extraction.*

"TAMPING" THE ESPRESSO COFFEE
(for all methods except the stovetop moka method)

"Tamping" is the compacting of the ground coffee in the machine's portafilter prior to brewing the Espresso coffee. Tamping is necessary since the water used to brew the Espresso is under pressure from the machine (8 to 10 times the weight of gravity) and will naturally find the path of least resistance through the coffee (not necessarily the road less traveled!). Interestingly enough, if the coffee finds loose channels to steep through, it will rush through these areas, taking the easy way out! If it does find the easy street, it overextracts the coffee surrounding the channels and underextracts the coffee in the channels. The resulting Espresso is bitter and astringent.

TAMPING TIPS:
- *Compact the coffee firmly and uniformly in the portafilter in order to force the water to flow through the coffee grounds in a manner which extracts the superior qualities of the coffee.*
- *The tamper (tool used to press down the Espresso coffee in the portafilter) should be applied to the coffee straight and head-on, NOT on an angle, since the level of the coffee will be inconsistent.*
- *Tamp the coffee four times in an "north, south, east and west" format on the inside diameter of the metal portafilter basket. This will evenly compact the coffee, giving the water a uniform bed to brew through.*
- *Packed down too light — the brewed Espresso coffee will be watered-down, lacking flavor and body.*
- *Packed down too tight — the brewed Espresso coffee will taste burnt.*
- *When the Espresso coffee is evenly packed down, beaming a clean polished and acceptable surface then the coffee-loaded portafilter can be mounted into the Espresso machine group head to begin brewing.*
- *The final assessment to the quality control of your tamping is the wet spent grounds, which determine the quality of coffee extraction. If "worm holes" are present in the wet coffee pack, then the water has found weak spots to channel through.*
- *When the wet spent grounds are knocked out of the portafilter, they should have the form of a "puck". If the knocked out spent coffee grounds fall out in the form of mush then the grind and the tamp were not correct.*
- *Essentially, it takes practice, practice and more practice to pack grounds perfectly.*

The thick, foaming milk isn't just poured into cups of waiting Espresso, it's dolloped and swooshed and scooped with spoons and spatulas, as a painter uses different brushes.

-JAN ANGILELLA, THE ART OF CAPPUCCINO IN BOLOGNA

CREAM OF THE CUP!

In the 1920s, everyone crooned along to the popular love song, "You're the Cream in My Coffee". Today, we could probably sing along to "You're the Topping on My No-Foam Double-Soy Decaf Latte". In this rapidly growing specialty coffee industry, coffee is not the only hot seller. Milk, in all its new and traditional forms, is also being consumed as a specialty beverage. In fact, my daughter Krista loves milk steamers.

Milk and cream are essential to the completion of our coffee creations. These include frothy cappuccinos and tall, steamy lattes which are made from a variety of all milk types, ranging from homogenized, down the milk fat scale to 1 percent and skim milk. (Some Espresso beverage drinkers now prefer lactose-free milk, soy, rice or "pseudomilk" to replace the milk in an Espresso-based beverage for personal health reasons.) There are many schools of thought for the type of milk to use, for the best frothing results. I've even had a restaurant owner who prepared her patrons' cappuccinos and lattes with half and half because it tasted richer!

These milk variations have generated a new-found Espresso vocabulary that is based on the fat content, quantity and style of milk served in the beverages, specifically: "skinny", "tall", "grande", "twiggy", "dry", "wet", etc. Then there are the elusive descriptions: "frothing, steaming, foaming, whatever!" It is easy to become frustrated by all these new terms.

With enough patience and finesse, the art of steaming and frothing (foaming) milk can be fun to learn in the comfort of your own kitchen. To begin, however, we need a clear understanding of some of the basic differences between:

STEAMED MILK: Milk which has been heated or scalded to just under the boiling point by the injection of steam or by a heat source. Aeration (or the incorporation of hot air) of the milk is minimal, so the milk's volume is unchanged, and it has only a small amount of froth (microbubbles).

FROTHED OR FOAMED MILK: Milk which has been both heated and aerated, by injecting a wand of hot steam at the surface of the milk. This creates a microfoam of tiny air bubbles, giving the milk an ideal consistency of very light whipped cream.

CLASSIC CAPPUCCINO: Typically it is made with Espresso combined with two kinds of heated milk, steamed and foamed. The classic recipe is one-third Espresso, one-third steamed milk and one-third foamed milk.

CAFFE LATTE: This Italian family's breakfast drink is made with one part Espresso coffee (in Italy, the Espresso is usually made with the stovetop moka apparatus) to two or three parts steamed milk. The milk is not foamed. (Generally the French call this drink a CAFÉ AU LAIT, but they add more milk and like to serve it in bowls.)

People prepare cappuccino and lattes in many different ways. In their own way each is correct.

TIPS FOR STEAMING AND FROTHING (FOAMING) MILK

TIPS FOR MILK:

Any liquid can be steamed, but achieving foamy frothy nirvana from milk is dependent on the protein and fat that milk contains. Fat is where the flavor and "mouthfeel" are, which is why in Italy they usually use whole milk. Whichever type of milk you prefer to use is the right one for you.

- Skim milk produces foam fastest, but with dry (no fun) stiff peaks called "dry foam".
- 1 % milk produces good results, and is a matter of preference.
- 2 % milk contains enough milk fat to enhance the flavor of the beverage and is the best, standard mid-range milk for the Espresso beverages offered in hotels and restaurants.

MOST IMPORTANT: In foaming milk everything should be cold; just as in brewing Espresso everything should be hot. Ice-cold milk microfoams or steams with better results.

TIPS FOR THE TOOLS:

There are a few budget or so-called "alternate frothing methods" for foaming milk, ranging from a plunger pot, or French-press coffee apparatus (as mentioned on page 45), to aerating milk in a saucepan on the stove with a flexible piano-wire whisk (see page 66, *Make a Basic Cappuccino or Latte Without a Machine*). For standard steaming/foaming methods, the following tools are recommended:

- A two-cup (500 mL) stainless steel container or frothing pitcher.
- A cooking thermometer (needle or digital) which reads up to 220°F (104°C).
- Optional foaming gadgets can be purchased, such as a stovetop steamer or a "steam toy", which can produce great foam and steamed milk.

PREPARATION TIPS:

- Before beginning, make sure all the equipment to be used has been cleaned and rinsed thoroughly since, as we all know, hot milk can breed bacteria. (This has always been a pet peeve with me). CLEANING TIP: A simple trick I always use/recommend for cleaning the steam wand is to soak the steam wand in hot, heavily salted water rather than vinegar water! Hot salt water breaks down the hardened calcified milk deposits which often "plug" up the steam wand, and also lead to mechanical problems if the milk buildup increases.
- Before using any manufacturer's home Espresso machine, please read the enclosed instructions carefully.
- Make sure the milk and the frothing pitcher are very cold.
- Always prepare the milk just before brewing the Espresso, to ensure that the beverage will be enjoyed at its hottest. (Heated milk can withstand waiting a minute or two better than Espresso can.)
- If you are using an Espresso machine, blow out any leftover condensed water or clogged milk solids by opening the steam valve into an empty container, then shut it off.

AN "ALTERNATIVE" FROTHING TECHNIQUE:

For an "alternative", simplified and economical technique for frothing milk, please refer to page 66 for tips from an Executive Chef on "How to Make a Basic Cappuccino or Latte Without a Machine!" or the plunger pot foaming tip on page 45.

TECHNIQUE FOR FOAMING/FROTHING MILK USING A STEAM WAND

This foaming/frothing technique uses approximately six to seven ounces (170 to 190 mL) of milk to make two cappuccinos.

FILL	the stainless steel frothing pitcher one-third full for foaming.
INSERT	or clip a cooking thermometer into the pitcher.
HOLD	the pitcher by its handle; place it under the steam wand or jet.
POSITION	the tip of the steam wand just beneath the surface of the milk.
OPEN	the steam valve fully.

TIPS:

- If the surface of the milk becomes "violent", and big bubbles form, then move the nozzle deeper into the liquid and turn down the steam a little.
- Look for small even bubbles. The goal is to aerate the milk to a satiny velvety texture.
- The "sounds" will be your navigation guide to foaming correctly.
  Wrong-way sounds: If it sounds like "blowing bubbles" through a straw then it is incorrect. This "bubble-bath" foam will quickly deflate. This signals that the steam wand is not positioned deep enough in the milk and you do not have enough steam pressure.
  Right-way sounds: A deep down "serious rumbling" sound is correct. The milk should also be increasing in volume.

DOUBLE	the milk in volume (and when the pitcher is hot to touch)
TURN OFF	the steam when the temperature hits 140°F (60°C). The temperature will continue to rise after you remove the milk from the heat. The maximum temperature should be 160°F (71°C). (Foamed milk will be a few degrees cooler than steamed milk since it incorporates air.)
WIPE	the nozzle thoroughly with a hot clean damp cloth. With your hands safely clear, turn the steam valve on to flush and clear out any milk in the wand.
NEVER	refoam the milk, ever! It contains too much condensed water.

TECHNIQUE FOR STEAMING MILK USING A STEAM WAND

This steaming technique heats the milk without foaming it.

FILL	the stainless steel pitcher two-thirds full for steaming.
INSERT	or clip a cooking thermometer into the pitcher.
HOLD	the pitcher by its handle; place it under the steam wand or jet.
BURY	the steam nozzle deep down, near the bottom of the pitcher, taking care not to scald the milk.
TURN	the steam wand off when the thermometer registers about 150 to 170°F (65 to 77°C) for steamed milk. (A simple rule to follow is that if the metal pitcher is too hot to hold comfortably for more than a second, then the milk will be too hot and will taste bad).
TAP	or gently bang the metal pitcher of steamed milk on the counter to get rid of the air. What's left is a thick, creamy milk that looks like whipped cream.

NEVER RESTEAM THE MILK!

The result is a foamy sculpture, high in the middle, concentric in the cup, and a slight border of light brown Espresso coffee, barely visible to the eye.

-JAN ANGILELLA, THE ART OF CAPPUCCINO IN BOLOGNA

ASSEMBLING BASIC ESPRESSO-BASED BEVERAGES

CLASSIC CAPPUCCINO
(Approximate proportions – one-third Espresso; one-third steamed milk; one-third foamed milk)

BREW   the Espresso coffee directly into the cup.

USE   a large spoon to block the foam at first so that initially hot milk pours out of the pitcher.

POUR   no more than a ½ cup (125 mL) of the steamed milk over the waiting Espresso.

SCOOP   and spoon and swoosh the foamy satiny sculpture, crowning the foamed milk at the top of the beverage.

MOCHACCINO
To make masterful mouth-watering mochaccinos, I have always preferred to add two to three ounces (60 to 90 mL) of a prepared rich chocolate syrup to the cold milk prior to foaming/frothing it. The thick, creamy chocolate syrup adds a rich texture to the milk and whips up beautifully with the steam from a steam wand.

Once the mocha foamed milk is added to the waiting Espresso, generously crown it with mounds of whipped cream and garnish with chocolate shavings, cinnamon and/or a maraschino cherry. If you prefer, you can use plain chocolate milk then follow the above instructions for making cappuccino.

CAFFE LATTE (or, in French, CAFÉ AU LAIT)
(Approximate Italian proportions – one part Espresso to four parts steamed milk, with no foam on top).

What is called a caffe latte in America is essentially a monster-sized cappuccino in Italy.

If you prefer to change the proportions to one part Espresso to four or six parts steamed milk, then you can call the drink whatever you wish!

BREW   the Espresso coffee directly into the cup.

POUR   the preferred proportion of steamed milk over the Espresso.

ADD   sugar or a biscotti, if desired.

CAFFE MACCHIATO

DOT   the middle of a cup of Espresso with just a tablespoon or two (15 to 30 mL) of the steamed milk, leaving a brown ring of Espresso around the edge of the cup.

That sounds like Satan making a cappuccino!

-ROSIE O'DONNELL REFERRING TO MADONNA'S VOCALS DURING A VOICE TRAINING EXERCISE.

HOW TO MAKE FOAMED/STEAMED MILK **WITHOUT** A MACHINE!

Often the simplest things are the most elusive. No need for expensive Expresso machines to make foamed milk for your cappuccinos. A simple whisk can be used to aerate the milk and a simple stoveburner as the heat source. In a few easy steps you can turn milk into rich, creamy, meringue-like froth to enjoy with your coffee. Soon you'll be coming off like the busy barista at your local coffee house, wowing your guests with wonderful cappuccinos!

Cold Milk	preferrably 2% or homogenized milk. (For quick measurements, fill one of the serving cups halfway with milk and multiply that amount by the number of people being served.)
Saucepan	small to medium-deep size
Whisk	flexible, loose-wired

FULL STEAM AHEAD!

POUR	COLD milk into saucepan. (The milk should only fill the pan halfway to allow for expanded foam.)
PLACE	saucepan and milk over medium to medium-high heat.
GRAB	your whisk and begin to stir the milk, slowly at first. (Loose, wide bubbles begin to form. The more you whisk the smaller and more condensed the foam becomes.)
INCREASE	whisk speed as milk temperature rises. WHISK the milk like you are beating eggs. (By beating patiently you will notice that the milk will begin to 'blossom' or 'swell'.)
DO NOT ALLOW MILK TO BOIL!	(Boiling the milk will spoil the foam and ruin the taste. If you think the milk is just about to boil then REMOVE the saucepan from the heat and continue to whisk.)
SET	the saucepan away from the heated stoveburner.
CONTINUE	to whisk until you have achieved the desired amount of milk foam.
SET	the foamed milk ambrosia aside for 30 seconds while you pour hot, freshly brewed coffee or Espresso into serving cups. During this time the milk will separate with the steamed (or scalded) milk settling to the bottom half of the pan and the light airy microbubbles of hot foamed milk will float to the top. The finished cappuccino is assembled with one-third coffee, one-third steamed milk and one-third foamed milk.

It is not the coffee I drink that makes me nervous – it's the coffee I DON'T HAVE to drink that makes me nervous!

-BEAT HEGNAUER, EXECUTIVE CHEF, THE BANFF CENTRE

"MAKE A BASIC CAPPUCCINO OR LATTE WITHOUT A MACHINE!"

TIPS FROM AN EXECUTIVE CHEF

For the past eight years Chef Beat Hegnauer has been an accredited Executive Chef at The Banff Centre in Banff, Alberta, Canada. In June 2000, he was invited to participate as an honorary coffee "schlurper", and tour a large coffee roasting facility in Portland, Oregon. His passion for coffee began as a young man growing up in Switzerland, when he discovered that coffee tasted better than milk! Over the years he has developed an appreciative taste for a quality cup of coffee.

During the past few years, when attending many Food Service demonstrations and trade shows, I was often approached by Chef Hegnauer as he questioned the need for my imported $1,500 supersonic electronic Espresso machine. He claimed that he could make a delicious basic cappuccino or latte without a fancy-schmancy Espresso machine. When I began to write this book, I decided to challenge Chef Hegnauer to demonstrate his basic machine-free method.

Chef Hegnauer explained that:

"Making Espresso coffee or creating cappuccinos and caffe lattes is similar to . . . cooking. One must keep in mind that the coffee beverage will only be as tasty as the quality of the ingredients used. The fresher and higher quality the coffee beans, the better flavor the finished coffee beverage will have."

Chef Hegnauer's favorite Espresso-making-method is his reliable moka-stovetop Espresso coffee pot. It consistently produces a satisfactory Espresso for him. He strongly advises that one should avoid the lesser-quality over-roasted Espresso coffee beans available on the market. The cheaper beans produce a bitter – not better – cup of Espresso coffee. When he needs to froth milk for cappuccinos and lattes, he religiously uses a back-to-basics "whisking" stovetop method, using only a whisk and milk in a saucepan.

Whether Chef Hegnauer is entertaining guests with dessert lattes or serving campfire cappuccinos for his family, he says these basic methods produce excellent results every time. He proclaims, "Making cappuccinos and lattes by these methods is so simple, anyone can do it!"

Chef Hegnauer's final suggestions are:

"Don't be intimidated or mesmerized by a given recipe. Use a recipe as a guide or as a fundamental basis of knowledge. Creatively expand on it and make your own creations – whether that is in cooking or making coffee creations!

CHEF HEGNAUER'S "WHISKED" FROTHED MILK

Frothed milk is so fluffy, you just can't "BEAT it"!

1 medium saucepan
1 flexible piano-wire whisk (not a stiff whisk)
7 oz. 2% (or homogenized) COLD milk   200 mL

POUR   cold milk into saucepan. Set on stove over medium heat and gently warm the milk.
WHISK   the milk in the saucepan CONSTANTLY and very BRISKLY while heating it.
CONTINUE   to whisk (aerate) the milk until it develops into a fluffy froth and almost doubles
                in volume. (A hand mixer can be used for quicker results).

DO NOT BOIL THE MILK. IF YOU DO BOIL IT, YOU WILL DESTROY THE FROTH. ONCE THE
FROTH IS DESTROYED YOU MUST DISCARD THE MILK AND START OVER AGAIN.

Pictured opposite

CHEF'S TIPS

* Chef Hegnauer recommends using your favorite Espresso coffee blend in a Moka-pot Stovetop
  Method (see page 51). He prefers this Espresso coffee-making method because it is simple,
  hassle-free and easy to clean up.
* When making an Espresso beverage, make sure the milk used for frothing is very cold, and the
  Espresso coffee is very hot.
* When assembling the cappuccino, Chef pours the steamed milk onto the waiting hot Espresso
  coffee, then spoons the fluffy milk froth on top. Voila! Yours to enjoy!

Cappuccino "Made WITHOUT a Machine", pictured opposite

Cappuccino "Fruit" Cocktail, page 78

Hot Cappuccino Cocktails

... for the Icy Days!

NO ONE CAN UNDERSTAND THE TRUTH UNTIL HE DRINKS
OF COFFEE'S FROTHY GOODNESS.

-SHEIK ABD-AL KADIR (1587)

Seven-Layered Espresso

This spectacular coffee is simply exquisite!

1 oz.	chocolate syrup	30 mL
1 oz.	hazelnut syrup	30 mL
3 oz.	steamed hot milk	90 mL
2-4 oz.	hot fresh Espresso	60-113 mL
	cocoa powder	

Into a tall, clear, tapered, tempered glass:

LAYER 1 ½ oz. (15 mL) of the chocolate syrup.

LAYER 2 ½ oz. (15 mL) of the hazelnut syrup.

LAYER 3 1½ oz. (45 mL) of the steamed milk
(add very slowly).

LAYER 4 ½ oz. (15 mL) chocolate syrup (pour very
slowly into the middle of the glass).

LAYER 5 ½ oz. (15 mL) hazelnut syrup (pour very
slowly into the middle of the glass.

LAYER 6 1½ oz. (45 mL) steamed milk (add very slowly).

LAYER 7 2-4 oz. of Espresso (pour into the middle very
slowly, the milk foam will layer itself).

SPRINKLE with cocoa powder.

Serves: 1

COFFEE SHOULD BE BLACK AS THE DEVIL, HOT AS HELL,
PURE AS AN ANGEL, AND AS SWEET AS LOVE.

-CHARLES MAURICE DE TALLEYRAND (1754-1838), 18TH CENTURY FRENCH STATESMAN,
DESCRIBING HIS CONCEPT OF A GOOD CUP OF COFFEE.

Black Forest Latte

For a traditional afternoon "Kaffeeklatsch"!

1¹/2 oz.	chocolate syrup (or crème de cacao liqueur)	45 mL
1¹/2 oz.	raspberry syrup (or Kirschwasser liqueur)	45 mL
2 oz.	hot fresh Espresso	60 mL
4-6 oz.	steamed milk	113-170 mL
	whipped cream	
¹/2 tsp.	raspberry syrup	2 mL
	shaved chocolate curls (or cocoa powder)	
	maraschino cherry	

POUR syrups (or liqueurs) into a 12-oz. (340 mL) latte mug or cup.

ADD the Espresso.

FILL with steamed milk.

STIR once around, lifting syrups up from bottom of mug or cup.

TOP with whipped cream.

Optional: Drizzle ¹/2 tsp. (2 mL) raspberry syrup on top of whipped cream.
Garnish with chocolate curls or sprinkle with cocoa powder.
Finish with a cherry on top!

INDULGE!

Serves: 1

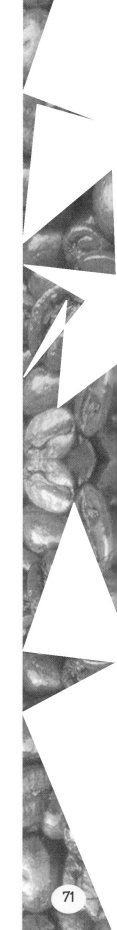

DRINK YOUR COFFEE, IT'S A JUNGLE OUT THERE!

-JANE TO TARZAN, 1911

(OR MAYBE IT WAS A "BLACK FOREST" OUT THERE!)

Millennium Mochaccino

For stellar coffee souls!

1½ oz.	unsweetened chocolate	45 mL
¼ cup	sugar	60 mL
4 oz.	hot fresh Espresso	113 mL
½ tsp.	ground cinnamon	2 mL
¾ cup	water	175 mL
2 cups	milk	500 mL
	whipped cream	

Optional: cinnamon sticks for garnish and stirring

COMBINE chocolate, sugar, Espresso, cinnamon and water in a medium saucepan over low heat.

STIR constantly until chocolate is melted and mixture is smooth.

HEAT just to boiling (not burning!).

REDUCE heat and simmer, uncovered, stirring constantly, for 4 minutes.

STIR in milk, heat thoroughly (DO NOT BOIL).

WHIP chocolate/milk mixture with a wire whisk until foamy.

POUR into mugs, top with whipped cream, and place cinnamon stick in cups for garnish, if desired.

Serves: 2-3

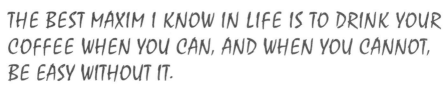

THE BEST MAXIM I KNOW IN LIFE IS TO DRINK YOUR COFFEE WHEN YOU CAN, AND WHEN YOU CANNOT, BE EASY WITHOUT IT.

-JONATHAN SWIFT (1667-1745), IRISH SATIRIST AND POET

Millionaire's Mochaccino

Dark, delightful and rich.

¹/₂ oz.	Grand Marnier	15 mL
¹/₂ oz.	Grand Marnier cream	15 mL
¹/₂ oz.	Kahlúa	15 mL
2-4 oz.	hot fresh Espresso	60-113 mL
4 oz.	steamed or foamed chocolate milk	113 mL

Optional: dollop of whipped cream
coffee beans

MIX all liqueurs in a tempered cappuccino mug or tempered glass mug.

ADD Espresso.

SPOON foamed milk on top of coffee mixture.

Optional:

TOP with a dollop of whipped cream.

SPRINKLE a few coffee beans on top of the whipped cream.

Optional: For a non-alcoholic beverage, substitute amaretto syrup or B-52 syrup for the liqueurs.

Serves: 1

COFFEE IS THE COMMON MAN'S GOLD, AND LIKE GOLD, IT BRINGS TO EVERY PERSON THE FEELING OF LUXURY AND NOBILITY.

-Sheik Abd-al-Kadir, In Praise of Coffee (1587)

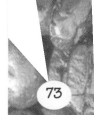

White Chocolate Cappuccino

Make sure the fireplace is on for this one!

4 oz.	light cream or whole milk	113 mL
1 oz.	good-quality chopped white chocolate	30 g
1 tsp.	brandy (or brandy syrup)	5 mL
1 tsp.	crème de cacao (liqueur or syrup)	5 mL
1/8 tsp.	vanilla	0.5 mL
3-4 oz.	hot fresh Espresso	90-113 mL
	whipped cream	
	chocolate curls or cocoa powder	

POUR cream (or milk) into medium saucepan; over medium heat, bring cream almost to boiling. Remove from heat.

ADD white chocolate; whisk until chocolate is completely melted and mixture is smooth.

WHISK in liqueurs (or syrups) and vanilla.

HEAT white chocolate mixture over low heat; whisk until frothy, about 1 minute.

POUR Espresso into a 14-oz. (390 mL) latte mug. Ladle white chocolate mixture over coffee.

TOP with whipped cream, chocolate curls or cocoa powder.

SERVE immediately.

Serves: 1

AH, THAT IS A PERFUME IN WHICH I DELIGHT: WHEN THEY ROAST COFFEE NEAR MY HOUSE, I HASTEN TO OPEN THE DOOR TO TAKE IN ALL THE AROMA.

-JEAN-JACQUES ROUSSEAU (1712-1778), FRENCH PHILOSOPHER AND WRITER

Black Gold Espresso

As good as gold!

2 oz.	hot fresh Espresso	60 mL
1 tsp.	crème de cacao (syrup or liqueur)	5 mL
1 oz.	rum flavoring (or rum)	30 mL
	soft whipped cream	

Optional: 1 oz. cognac.

POUR all liquids into a stemmed tempered cocktail glass, or a 6-oz. (170 mL) cappuccino mug.

TOP with a dollop of soft whipped cream.

SERVE hot!

Optional: Add cognac if desired.

Serves: 1

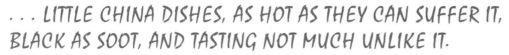

. . . LITTLE CHINA DISHES, AS HOT AS THEY CAN SUFFER IT, BLACK AS SOOT, AND TASTING NOT MUCH UNLIKE IT.

-A TRAVELER IN THE EARLY 16TH CENTURY, WRITING ABOUT TURKS DRINKING COFFEE

Royal Mochaccino

Divinely different.

4 tsp.	chocolate syrup	20 mL
1/2 cup	milk or light cream	125 mL
3/4 tsp.	cinnamon	3 mL
1/4 tsp.	nutmeg	1 mL
1 tbsp.	white sugar	15 mL
12 oz.	hot fresh Espresso	340 mL

PUT 1 tsp. (15 mL) chocolate syrup into each of 4 cups.

FROTH milk or cream until double in volume.

ADD 1/4 tsp (1 mL) cinnamon, nutmeg and sugar.

STIR remaining 1/2 tsp. (2 mL) cinnamon into hot Espresso.

POUR Espresso into cups.

STIR chocolate syrup and Espresso together.

TOP coffee with frothed milk or cream mixture.

Serves: 4

WITHOUT THE JOY OF JAVA, LIFE DOESN'T AMOUNT TO A "HILL OF BEANS"!

-ANONYMOUS

Orange-Kissed Mochaccino

The zest of orange and the richness of mochaccino!

2 cups	cold milk	500 mL
4 oz.	chocolate syrup	113 mL
4 oz.	hot fresh Espresso	113 mL
1-2	oranges, quartered	1-2
1/8 tsp.	ground cinnamon	0.5 mL
1/4 tsp.	grated orange peel	1 mL

POUR cold milk, then syrup, into frothing jug. Froth with steam wand until syrup and milk are well blended into a hot chocolate froth.

POUR Espresso into 2, 12-oz. (340 mL) mugs.

SQUEEZE juice from orange wedges into freshly made Espresso. Discard orange wedges.

STIR cinnamon into Espresso-orange blend.

POUR hot chocolate froth into Espresso mixture.

GARNISH with a dash of cinnamon and sprinkle lightly with grated orange peel.

Serves: 2

THE COMBINED AROMA OF ORANGES, CHOCOLATE AND COFFEE IN BEVERAGES IS AROUSING, EXCITING AND UNFORGETTABLE.

-ANONYMOUS

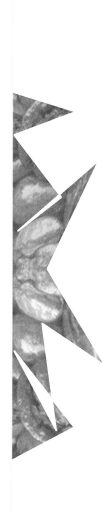

Cappuccino "Fruit" Cocktail

A new "fruit cocktail" fashion!

2 tsp.	berry fruit marmalade	10 mL
	(preferably a raspberry mixture)	
	hot fresh Espresso	
	whipped cream	
	fresh berries for garnish	

Optional: 1 oz. (30 mL) fruit/berry liqueur or syrup(s)

PLACE 2 tsp. (10 mL) marmalade into a heat-resistant coffee dessert glass.

POUR Espresso over fruit marmalade.

GARNISH with whipped cream and top with whole berries.

SERVE with a dessert coffee spoon to stir the tasty flavors together.

Optional: Drizzle fruit/berry liqueurs or syrup(s) over the whipped cream and berries.

Serves: 1

Pictured on page 68.

THE ADDICTIVE INGREDIENTS: RASPBERRIES, CHOCOLATE AND COFFEE HAVE BEEN INCORPORATED INTO RICH DESSERTS FOR YEARS. THIS BEVERAGE DESSERT HAS BEEN DERIVED FROM A TRADITIONAL ITALIAN DESSERT RECIPE.

Dutch Mocha Mint Latte

A heavenly dessert beverage.

1³/₄ oz.	chocolate syrup	50 mL
¹/₂ oz.	crème de menthe (liqueur or syrup)	15 mL
¹/₂ oz.	crème de cacao (liqueur or syrup)	15 mL
2 oz.	hot fresh Espresso	60 mL
6 oz.	hot steamed or foamed milk	170 mL
	whipped cream	
	cocoa powder	
	shaved chocolate	

POUR chocolate syrup, liqueurs (or syrups) and Espresso into a large (12-oz./340 mL or so) latte mug.

FILL with hot steamed or foamed milk.

STIR once, lifting from the bottom to bring up the syrup, liqueurs and coffee.

TOP with whipped cream.

SPRINKLE with cocoa powder and shaved chocolate.

Serves: 1

COFFEE HAS TWO VIRTUES. IT IS WET AND IT IS WARM.

-OLD DUTCH SAYING

Italian Delight Espresso

This one will have you so wired – you'll pick up AM radio!

¹/₄-¹/₂ oz.	almond syrup (or amaretto liqueur)	7-15 mL
2-4 oz.	hot fresh Espresso	60-113 mL
	whipped cream	

Optional:	¹/₂-1 oz. sambuca liqueur	15-30 mL

POUR   syrup (or liqueur) into a glass mug.
ADD   Espresso.
TOP   with a dollop of whipped cream.

SALUT!

Serves: 1

Espresso Ecstasy

Nectar of the gods.

2-4 oz.	hot fresh Espresso	60-113 mL
2-4 oz.	light cream	60-113 mL
1 tsp.	white sugar	5 mL

POUR   Espresso into a cappuccino mug.
MIX   cream with sugar.
ADD   to Espresso.

Serves: 1

ESPRESSO IS TO ITALY WHAT CHAMPAGNE IS TO FRANCE.

CHARLES MAURICE DE TALLEYRAND (1754-1838), 18TH CENTURY FRENCH STATESMAN, DESCRIBING HIS CONCEPT OF A GOOD CUP OF COFFEE.

Turtle Mochaccino

For you turtle lovers!

2 oz.	hot fresh Espresso (or strong coffee)	60 mL
1 oz.	caramel syrup	30 mL
1 oz.	macadamia syrup (or hazelnut or Frangelico)	30 mL
1 oz.	chocolate syrup	30 mL
6 oz.	steamed milk	170 mL

COMBINE Espresso and all syrups in a 12-oz. (340 mL) latte mug or tall tempered glass.

FILL the rest of the mug or glass with the steamed milk.

Serves: 1

Crème de Caramel Cappuccino

The crème de la crème of cappos.

2 oz.	hot fresh Espresso	60 mL
1 oz.	vanilla syrup (or amaretto cream liqueur)	30 mL
5-7 oz.	foamed or frothed milk	145-200 mL
	thick caramel syrup	

POUR Espresso into a latte or cappuccino mug; add the vanilla syrup.

FILL the rest of the way with frothed milk, then spoon some extra foamed milk on top.

DRIZZLE caramel syrup over the foam.

ENJOY!

Serves: 1

OH, FORTUNATE ARE THOSE WHOSE HEARTS HAVE OFTEN BEEN WARMED BY THIS SWEET DRINK!

-GUILLAUME MASSIEU (1665-1722)

Midnight Cappuccino

A nightcap to drift away with.

1¹/₂ tbsp.	chocolate syrup (or crème de cacao liqueur)	22 mL
1¹/₂ tbsp.	sambuca	22 mL
2 oz.	hot fresh Espresso (or strong coffee)	60 mL
	soft whipped cream	

POUR the syrup (or liqueur) and the sambuca into a mug.

ADD the Espresso.

TOP with a dollop of the whipped cream.

SERVE immediately.

Optional: Omit sambuca if you prefer a non-alcoholic beverage.

Serves: 1

GOOD COMMUNICATION IS AS STIMULATING AS BLACK COFFEE, AND JUST AS HARD TO SLEEP AFTER.

-ANNE MORROW LINDBERGH (1906-2001)

Brown Cow Cappuccino

A "Moo"-ving beverage experience.

Allow the beverage to settle for a few seconds and watch layers form – for a proud presentation to your guests – or a treat for yourself!

4-6 oz.	hot steamed/foamed milk	113-170 mL
2 oz.	hot fresh Espresso	60 mL
½-1 oz.	Kahlúa (or B-52 syrup)	15-30 mL
½-1 oz.	white crème de cacao (or white chocolate syrup)	15-30 mL

POUR the milk into your favorite stemmed tall glass mug.

POUR the hot Espresso and the liqueurs very slowly, on an angle, down the side of the mug.

Serves: 1

"It's true, I did jump over the moon.
I had waaaaay too much coffee that day!"

Cowboy Cappuccino©

Coming from "Cowtown", I had to include this!
The most famous cappuccino you've never "HERD" of!

1	tin cup	1
1/2 pot	campfire coffee (the stronger the better!)	1/2 pot
1	brown cow (well rested)	1
	sugar if desired	

FILL the cup half full with hot black coffee.

POSITION yourself CAREFULLY beside a very relaxed cow.

SQUEEZE one of the cow's teats gently (while holding the coffee cup under the udder) until warm foamed milk comes out.

CONTINUE milking until cup is full and frothy.

ADD sugar if desired.

Optional: 2 oz. (60 mL) of Jack Daniels or rum may be added.

Serves: 1

Pictured opposite.

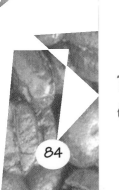

THERE IS NO SUCH THING AS COFFEE THAT'S TOO STRONG, ONLY PEOPLE WHO ARE WEAK!

-THE COFFEE COWBOY - SITTING BY HIS CAMPFIRE

Cowboy Cappuccino

"Larger-Than-Life" Latte

"Larger-Than-Life" Latte

Fast, easy and simple, simple, simple!

12 cups	water	3 L
11 scoops*	good-quality strong ground coffee	11 scoops
1¹/₂ cups	light cream	375 mL
³/₄ cup	sugar	175 mL

BREW   coffee in a 12-cup (3 L) coffee maker, using
the water and coffee.

While coffee is brewing . . .

HEAT   the cream and sugar almost to boiling in
a saucepan.

PUT   the hot cream and sugar into an extra-large
thermal carafe.

POUR   the coffee into the carafe.

Serves: 12

* 1 scoop of coffee is approximately 2 tbsp. (30 mL).

Pictured opposite.

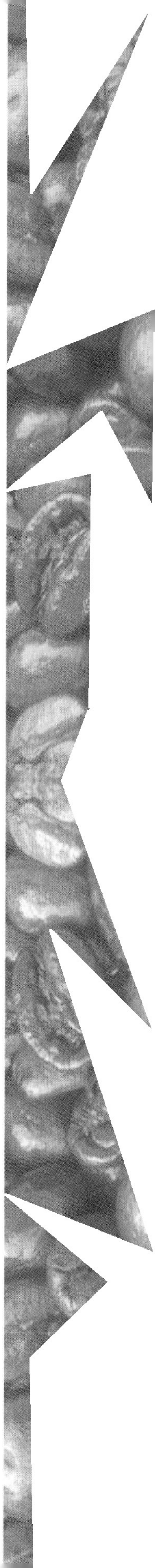

THE COFFEE IS PREPARED IN SUCH A WAY THAT IT MAKES THOSE WHO DRINK IT WITTY . . .

-BARON DE LA BRÈDE ET DE MONTESQUIEU (1689-1755), FRENCH POLITICAL PHILOSOPHER

Toffee Coffee Latte

The coffee-lover's candy.

¹/₄ oz.	banana (syrup or liqueur)	7 mL
¹/₄ oz.	hazelnut syrup (or Frangelico)	7 mL
¹/₄ oz.	caramel or English toffee syrup	7 mL
2 oz.	hot fresh Espresso (or strong coffee)	60 mL
5-6 oz.	hot steamed milk	145-170 mL

Optional: ground hazelnuts for topping.

POUR all flavored syrups (or liqueurs) into a 12-oz. (340 mL) latte mug.

ADD the Espresso

ADD the hot steamed milk

STIR once around, lifting upward to bring up syrups.

Optional: Dust with ground hazelnuts.

Serves: 1

Pictured on page 17.

BETTER 'LATTE' THAN NEVER!

-ANONYMOUS

B-52 Mocha Au Lait

A shot of super delicious!

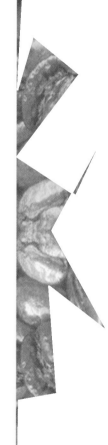

4-6 oz.	milk or light cream	113-170 mL
2 oz.	chocolate syrup	60 mL
4-6 oz.	hot fresh Espresso	113-170 mL
2-3 oz.	B-52 syrup (or B-52 liqueurs)	60-90 mL
	cocoa powder	

FILL a mug halfway with milk or light cream.

ADD chocolate syrup.

STEAM the chocolate and milk mixture together, in the cup, with a steam wand, until DOUBLED in volume.

FILL the mug the rest of the way with Espresso.

STIR IN the B-52 syrup (or B-52 liqueurs – 1/3 each Grand Marnier, Kahlúa and Bailey's).

SPRINKLE with cocoa powder.

LAST COMES THE BEVERAGE OF THE ORIENT SHORE, MOCHA, FAR OFF . . . AND DIGESTION WAITS ON PLEASURE AS YOU SIP.

-POPE LEO XII (1760-1820), SHORT ODE TO THE BREW IN *FRUGALITY*

Amaretto Mochaccino

Divinely decadent!

1-2 oz.	chocolate syrup	30-60 mL
4-5 oz.	hot steamed milk	113-145 mL
2 oz.	hot fresh Espresso	15 mL
1/2 oz.	almond syrup (or amaretto liqueur)	15 mL
	soft whipped cream	

FOAM/FROTH chocolate syrup and milk together, in a 12-oz. (340 mL) cappuccino mug or tempered glass mug. (If a frothing jug is used, then pour into mug once frothing is completed.)

SLOWLY ADD Espresso and syrup (or liqueur) to foamed chocolate milk.

TOP with a dollop of whipped cream.

Serves: 1

Tip: If a glass mug is used, allow finished beverage to settle. Separate layers will form, which produces an eye-appealing presentation.

Pictured on page 18.

TO DRINK IS HUMAN, TO DRINK MOCHACCINO IS DIVINE!

-ANONYMOUS

Cappuccino au Cointreau

Il flavor intenso!

½-1 oz.	Cointreau (or orange syrup)	15-30 mL
1	clove	1
	small piece of orange peel	
½-1 oz.	rum	15-30 mL
2 oz.	hot fresh Espresso	60 mL
4-6 oz.	hot foamed milk	113-170 mL
	whipped cream	
	grated orange peel	

PLACE the clove, Cointreau, orange peel and the rum in a saucepan.

HEAT gently, just enough to "warm" the liquids.

REMOVE from the heat and discard the clove.

ADD the Espresso.

POUR into a heat-resistant glass or cup immediately.

POUR the milk into the Espresso and stir gently.

TOP with whipped cream.

SPRINKLE with grated orange peel.

Optional: Remove the rum if you prefer a non-alcoholic beverage.

Serves: 1

HERE'S YOUR COFFEE, SIR . . . IT DOESN'T TAKE MUCH TO MAKE IT: PUT IN THE RIGHT MEASURE AND DON'T SPILL IT ON THE FLAME. LET THE FROTH RISE, THEN QUICKLY TURN IT DOWN.

-CARLO GOLDONI (1707-1793), THE PRUSSIAN BRIDE.

Electric Espresso

Coffee with a shocking "byte"!

½ oz.	dark crème de cacao	15 mL
½ oz.	white crème de cacao	15 mL
2-4 oz.	hot fresh Espresso	60-113 mL
	whipped cream	

POUR liqueurs into a 6-oz. (170 mL) cappuccino mug.
ADD the hot Espresso.
TOP with a dollop of whipped cream.

Optional: Substitute ½ oz. (15 mL) each of dark and white chocolate syrups, for the liqueurs.

Serves: 1

Pictured on page 189.

TOO MUCH COFFEE - NOT ENOUGH HARD DRIVE!

-Anonymous

Soya-ccino Cocktail

The healthy alternative cappuccino!

4-6 oz.	cold soymilk (or rice milk)	113-170 mL
2-4 oz.	hot fresh Espresso	60-113 mL

FROTH/FOAM soymilk (or rice milk) before pouring it into your favorite 12-oz. (340 mL) latte or cappuccino mug.

POUR Espresso slowly into foamed soymilk.

CHEERS, to the best of health!

Serves: 1

Cocoa-Cabana Cappuccino

Go bananas over this one!

3-4 oz.	hot fresh Espresso	90-113 mL
1 oz.	crème de cacao (liqueur or syrup)	30 mL
1 oz.	crème de banana (liqueur or syrup)	30 mL
8 oz.	steamed milk	250 mL

MIX the Espresso and liqueurs (or syrups) together in a latte mug.

FILL the mug with the steamed milk.

SERVE immediately.

Serves: 1

O COFFEE . . . THOU GIVEST HEALTH TO THOSE WHO LABOR, AND ENABLEST THE GOOD TO FIND THE TRUTH.

-SHEIK ABD-AL-KADIR

"Rolo"-Way Latte

Let this sweet blend "rolo" you away!

³/₄ oz.	chocolate syrup	20 mL
³/₄ oz.	caramel syrup	20 mL
2 oz.	hot fresh Espresso	60 mL
4 oz.	steamed hot milk	113 mL
	soft whipped cream	
	caramel syrup	
	cocoa powder	

POUR the syrups into a cappuccino mug.

ADD the hot Espresso.

STIR only once.

POUR the milk on top of the Espresso.

TOP with a dollop of whipped cream.

DRIZZLE the whipped cream with caramel (and maybe a touch of chocolate too!) syrup.

DUST with cocoa powder.

Serves: 1

GLASBERGEN

Stress Management Tip # 213:
When work becomes unbearable, grab the steam
from your coffee and let it carry you away.

Kahlúa Cream Cappuccino

A delight in every sip!

½ oz.	Kahlúa or (chocolate syrup)	15 mL
1-2 oz.	white crème de cacao (or white chocolate syrup)	30-60 mL
2 oz.	hot fresh Espresso	60 mL
4 oz.	hot steamed or foamed milk	120 mL
	whipped cream	
	cocoa powder	

POUR   all liqueurs (or syrups) into a tall stemmed glass.

ADD   the Espresso.

SPOON   milk on top of coffee mixture.

TOP   with a dollop of whipped cream.

DUST   with cocoa powder.

Serves: 1

ONE SIP OF THIS WILL BATHE DROOPING SPIRITS IN DELIGHT BEYOND THE BLISS OF DREAMS.

-JOHN MILTON (1608-1674)

95

Cappuccino Cream Dream

For an afternoon "escape" break.

4 oz.	milk or light cream	113 mL
2 oz.	hot fresh Espresso	60 mL
½ oz.	chocolate syrup (or crème de cacao liqueur)	15 mL
½ oz.	white chocolate syrup (or white crème de cacao liqueur)	15 mL
	whipped cream	
	cocoa powder	

FROTH milk until double in volume and frothy.

POUR Espresso into a cappuccino mug.

DOLLOP foamed milk into Espresso in mug.

POUR liqueurs (or syrups) into the middle of the foamed milk.

LAYER whipped cream on top of milk and dust with cocoa powder.

Serves: 1

WHAT YOU NEED IN LIFE IS A GOOD "PERK" ME UP!

-ANONYMOUS

Irish Cream
Cappuccino Cocktail

The idea is to sip hot cappuccino through chilled whipped cream.

1/4-1/2 oz.	Irish cream syrup (or Irish whiskey)	7-15 mL
1/4-1/2 oz.	crème de menthe (syrup or liqueur)	7-15 mL
1/4-1/2 oz.	orange syrup (or Grand Marnier)	7-15 mL
4 oz.	hot foamed/frothed milk	113 mL
2 oz.	hot fresh Espresso	60 mL
	chilled whipped cream	

POUR all syrups (or liqueurs) into a 12-oz. (341 mL) cappuccino mug or tall tempered glass stem mug.

ADD hot milk.

STIR IN Espresso.

TOP with mounds of chilled whipped cream.

Serves: 1

ONLY IRISH COFFEE PROVIDES IN A SINGLE GLASS ALL FOUR ESSENTIAL FOOD GROUPS: ALCOHOL, CAFFEINE, SUGAR AND FAT!

-ALEX LEVINE

Cognac Mochaccino

Surprisingly light – shamefully rich!

1 oz.	cognac	30 mL
1 tsp.	sugar	5 mL
2 oz.	hot fresh Espresso	60 mL
1/2 cup	prepared hot chocolate	125 mL
4 oz.	milk or light cream	113 mL
	grated chocolate	

STIR together the cognac, sugar, Espresso and hot chocolate.

REHEAT gently. DO NOT BOIL.

FROTH 4 oz. (113 mL) milk until doubled in volume.

POUR the Espresso mixture into 2 tempered cognac glasses or latte mugs.

DOLLOP frothed milk over the Espresso.

SPRINKLE grated chocolate on top.

Optional: Cognac may be replaced with syrup of choice for a non-alcoholic beverage.

Serves: 1

INTOXICATING, ADDICTIVE AND PERFECTLY LEGAL!

-ANONYMOUS

Cognac 'n' Cream Cappuccino

Elegant, yet so easy to make.

4 oz.	milk	113 mL
2 oz.	hot fresh Espresso	60 mL
½ oz.	cognac	15 mL
½ oz.	orange syrup (or Grand Marnier cream or Bailey's)	15 mL

FROTH   milk until doubled in volume, foamed and frothy.

POUR   Espresso into a cappuccino mug.

DOLLOP   foamed milk over Espresso in mug.

ADD   cognac and orange syrup and stir gently.

SERVE   immediately!

Optional: Irish cream syrup may replace cognac for a non-alcoholic recipe.

Serves: 1

GRAB LIFE BY THE BEANS!

-JUAN VALDEZ

After Eight Mint Cappuccino

Watch your guests crowd around this one!

1 oz.	crème de cacao (liqueur or syrup)	30 mL
1 oz.	crème de menthe (liqueur or syrup)	30 mL
2-4 oz.	hot fresh Espresso	60-113 mL
	chocolate curls	
	chocolate-mint wafers	

COMBINE all ingredients, except chocolate curls and wafers, in a cappuccino mug.

GARNISH with chocolate curls.

SERVE immediately with thin chocolate-mint wafers on the side.

Serves: 1

COFFEE HAS COME INTO GENERAL USE AS A FOOD IN THE MORNING, AND AFTER DINNER AS AN EXHILARATING AND TONIC DRINK.

-(JEAN) ANTHELME BRILLAT-SAVARIN (1755-1826), FRENCH JURIST AND GOURMET, THE PHYSIOLOGY OF TASTE

Iced
Cappuccino
Cocktails

. . . for the Hot Days!

ICED COFFEE AND CAPPUCCINO DRINKS
PICK UP WHERE MILKSHAKES LEAVE OFF!

-TOM PEIKO, BEVMARK CONSULTANT

Fake -a- Frappéccino

Tastes like the real thing!

4 oz.	cold Espresso (or strong coffee)	113 mL
2-3 oz.	chocolate syrup	60-90 mL
½ tbsp.	vanilla syrup	7 mL
4 oz.	milk	113 mL
3 cups	crushed ice, approximately	750 mL
	mounds of whipped cream	
	small pieces of chocolate	

PLACE all the ingredients, except whipped cream and chocolate pieces, in a blender and blend until the ice is thoroughly crushed.

POUR into a large, tall chilled glass.

GARNISH with mounds of whipped cream and small pieces of chocolate.

Serves: 1

Pictured opposite.

TASTES SO GREAT YOU WON'T KNOW IT'S A FAKE!

Fake -a- Frappéccino

Iced Black Forest Mochaccino

Iced Black Forest Mochaccino

Formally, as I know it, Tante Maria's "Eiskaffee"!

2-4 oz.	cold Espresso (or strong coffee)	60-113 mL
1 tbsp.	chocolate syrup (or crème de cacao)	15 mL
1 tbsp.	cherry (or raspberry) syrup	15 mL
	(or Kirschwasser – German cherry Schnaps)	
1-2 scoops	vanilla or coffee ice cream	1-2 scoops
	whipped cream	
	chocolate curls (or sprinkles)	
	maraschino cherry	

POUR   Espresso into a tall 12-oz. (340 mL)
glass or milkshake server.

ADD   syrups (or liqueurs) and ice cream.

TOP   with a generous dollop of whipped cream.

GARNISH with chocolate curls and a cherry!

Serves: 1

Variation: Drizzle crème de menthe (liqueur or syrup) on
top of the whipped cream.

Pictured opposite.

AFTER A FEW MONTH'S ACQUAINTANCE WITH EUROPEAN
COFFEE . . . HE BEGINS TO WONDER IF THE RICH
BEVERAGE OF HOME, WITH ITS CLOTTED LAYER OF CREAM
ON TOP OF IT, IS NOT A MERE DREAM AFTER ALL, BUT A
THING WHICH NEVER EXISTED!

-MARK TWAIN (SAMUEL CLEMENS), (1835-1910), US NOVELIST AND HUMORIST

Coffee-Break Shake

Deliciously nutritious!

½ cup	cold strong coffee (or Espresso)	125 mL
3 tbsp.	malted milk powder	45 mL
	(e.g., Ovaltine – natural or chocolate flavor)	
2 tsp.	sugar	10 mL
¼ cup	milk	60 mL
1	ripe medium banana, peeled, chunked	1
4	ice cubes	4

Optional: dash of cinnamon for garnish

PLACE coffee, malted milk powder, sugar and milk into a blender.

ADD banana and ice cubes.

BLEND on high for approximately ½ minute, until thick and frothy.

POUR into a tall glass.

Optional: Sprinkle with cinnamon if desired.

Serves: 1

THE MORNING COFFEE HAS AN EXHILARATION ABOUT IT WHICH THE CHEERING INFLUENCE OF THE AFTERNOON CUP OF TEA CANNOT BE EXPECTED TO REPRODUCE.

-OLIVER WENDELL HOLMES, SR. (1809-1894), US PHYSICIAN AND POET

Espresso-Cocoa Cooler

Rich and delicious!

2-3 tsp.	chocolate syrup	10-15 mL
4 oz.	milk	113 mL
8 oz.	cold Espresso	250 mL
1/2 tsp.	vanilla	2 mL
	sweetened whipped cream	

MIX chocolate syrup with milk until syrup is dissolved.
COMBINE cold coffee, chocolate milk and vanilla.
POUR over ice in tall chilled glasses.
TOP each with whipped cream.

Serves: 2

Iced Yogurt-ccino

A healthy refresher that's delicious anytime!

3-4 oz.	cold Espresso	90-113 mL
3/4 cup	non-fat frozen yogurt	175 mL
1/2 cup	ice cubes	125 mL
1 1/2 tbsp.	sugar	22 mL

PLACE all ingredients into a blender and whirl until smooth and thoroughly blended.
POUR into a tall glass and serve immediately.

Serves: 1

IT IS THEIR GREAT COFFEE DRINKING THAT GAVE ONE THE ADMIRABLE CLARITY, AND THE OTHER THE FERVENT HARMONY OF HIS STYLE.

-(JEAN) ANTHELME BRILLAT-SAVARIN (1755-1826), FRENCH JURIST AND GOURMET

Good-For-You Cappuccino Cooler

Nutritious snack or dessert.

2 x 6 oz.	containers fat-free cappuccino yogurt (organic, if you prefer)	2 x 170 mL
1 cup	fat-free milk (organic, if you prefer)	250 mL
2 cups	low-fat ice cream, mocha or coffee flavor cocoa powder or cinnamon	500 mL

PLACE all ingredients, except cocoa or cinnamon, in a blender and blend until smooth.

POUR into glasses.

SPRINKLE with cocoa or cinnamon, if desired.

Serves: 4

Variation: soymilk or rice milk may be substituted for milk, RICE DREAM™ may be substituted for ice cream.

SPANDEX IS TO THE BODY, WHAT COFFEE IS TO THE MIND.

-ANONYMOUS

"Fast-Slim" Cappuccino Shake

This recipe comes from a "not-so-skinny" chef!

11 oz.	can Slim-Fast™ (any flavor)	325 mL
2 oz.	cold Espresso (or strong coffee)	60 mL

PLACE Slim-Fast™, and Espresso in a blender.
BLEND until smooth and slightly frothy.
POUR into a large glass.

Serves: 1

Variation: For a hot drink, froth Slim-Fast™, then add to
hot Espresso.

Thanks Clay Frotten!

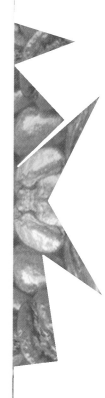

Nirvana Espresso Shake

From nervosa to nirvana in just a shake!

3-4 oz.	cold Espresso coffee	90-113 mL
1 oz.	amaretto (syrup or liqueur)	30 mL
3 oz.	yogurt (or yogurt drink)	90 mL
2 cups	crushed ice	500 mL
	chocolate whipped cream (see page 158)	

BLEND all ingredients, except the chocolate whipped
cream, in a blender until smooth.
SERVE in a 16-oz. (500 mL) glass.
TOP with chocolate whipped cream.

Serves: 1 tall

MAY I HAVE A DOUBLE-TALL HALF-CAFF SKINNY LATTE
PLEASE! (GO FIGURE!)

Brain Freeze Cappuccino Cooler

Don't drink this too fast or you might get an ice-cream headache!

1/2	large banana (or 1 small banana)	1/2
2 oz.	cold Espresso	60 mL
1 scoop	coffee ice cream	1 scoop
3/4 cup	ice	175 mL
	whipped cream	
	chocolate shavings	

PLACE all ingredients, except the whipped cream and shaved chocolate, in a blender and blend until smooth.

POUR into a large glass.

TOP with whipped cream and shaved chocolate.

Serves: 1

YOU DRINK SO MUCH ESPRESSO, YOUR EYES STAY OPEN WHEN YOU SNEEZE!

Iced Thai Coffee

Decadently different.

1¹/₂ cups	cold Espresso (or strong coffee)	375 mL
1 tbsp.	sweetened condensed milk	15 mL
1 tbsp.	brown sugar	15 mL
dash	each of cinnamon and ground cloves	dash

Optional: light cream

STIR   into the coffee, the sweetened condensed milk,
brown sugar, cinnamon and ground cloves.

POUR   the coffee mixture into a tall glass, over ice,
stirring to blend.

Optional: Add light cream if desired.

Serves: 1

FACT . . . THAI COFFEE IS AVAILABLE IN AN EXTREMELY STRONG
VERSION CALLED "OLIANG". AN OLIANG BRAND NAME CALLED
"PANTAINORASINGH" IS MADE OF 50% COFFEE, 25% CORN,
20% SOYABEAN AND 5% SESAME SEED !!

Cappuccino Smoothie

Freshly blended smoothies can be enjoyed after dinner with friends or family, or as a quiet treat for yourself.

2 cups	cold Espresso (or strong coffee)	500 mL
2 cups	coffee-flavored ice cream or sorbet	500 mL
1¼ cups	milk	300 mL
6 cups	chopped ice	1.5 L
	whipped cream	
	ground cinnamon	
	cocoa powder	

PLACE Espresso, ice cream, milk and ice in a blender and blend until smooth.

POUR into stemmed coffee or ice-cream glasses.

TOP with a dollop of whipped cream and sprinkle with cinnamon and cocoa.

Serves: 6

For Mocha Cappuccino Smoothies:
Substitute chocolate ice cream for the coffee-flavored ice cream, and chocolate milk for the regular milk. Garnish with chocolate shavings.

I'LL HAVE A DOUBLE CAPPUCCINO, HALF-CAF, NON-FAT MILK, WITH ENOUGH FOAM TO BE AESTHETICALLY PLEASING, BUT NOT SO MUCH THAT IT WILL LEAVE A MOUSTACHE!

-NILES CRANE, FRASIER

Mocha Coffee Float

A fluffy fizzy coffee float - full of flavor!

3 tbsp.	coffee syrup (see page 150)	45 mL
2 tbsp.	milk	30 mL
½ tsp.	vanilla	2 mL
2 scoops	good-quality coffee ice cream	2 scoops
½ cup	soda water or sparkling mineral water	125 mL
	whipped cream	
	chocolate shavings	

POUR the coffee syrup, milk and vanilla into a tall chilled glass. Stir with a spoon.

PLACE the ice cream on top of the milk.

FILL the glass with soda water.

STIR gently, then top with whipped cream and chocolate shavings.

Serves: 1

A YOUNG LADY IN A COFFEEHOUSE ASKED, "MAY I HAVE A LATTE WITH NOT VERY MUCH MILK?!?"

Amaretto Iced Smoothie

This one is for the young — in years or at heart.

½ oz.	amaretto (syrup or liqueur)	15 mL
½ oz.	Kahlúa	15 mL
6 oz.	cold Espresso (or strong coffee)	170 mL
1-1½ scoops	chocolate ice cream	1-1½ scoops
	whipped cream	
	chocolate shavings	

PUT   syrup, liqueur, Espresso and ice cream in a blender and blend until smooth.

TOP   with whipped cream and chocolate shavings.

SERVE   immediately.

Optional: For a real treat, serve this with decadent cappuccino-filled cookie straws.

for a non-alcoholic beverage, omit the Kahlúa.

Serves: 1

DRINKING TOO MUCH COFFEE CAN CAUSE A LATTE PROBLEM - NEVER INTRODUCE YOUR SPOUSE AS YOUR COFFEE-MATE!

Cookies 'n' Cream Iced Cappuccino

Mr. Christie you make good . . . cappuccinos!

2-4 oz.	cold Espresso	60-113 mL
1/2 cup	milk	125 mL
2-3	Oreo cookies (or black cookies with white cream filling)	2-3
1 1/4 cups	crushed ice	300 mL

Optional: chocolate shavings

POUR Espresso, milk and cookies into a blender container.
ADD ice cubes.
BLEND until smooth.

Optional: Increase or decrease amount of milk for desired consistency.

SERVE with fat straws in a tall glass.

Optional: Top with chocolate shavings.

Serves: 1

YESTERDAY'S LEFTOVER ESPRESSO (OR STRONG BREWED COFFEE) CAN BE STORED IN A COVERED CONTAINER FOR A DAY OR TWO. USE IT IN ANY OF THESE REFRESHING ICED CAPPUCCINOS. DRINK UP!

Spicy-Icy Coffee Cocktail

A spicy touch for those who take their coffee black!

13-15 oz.	cold strong coffee (or Espresso)	370-425 mL
1/4 tsp.	cinnamon	1 mL
	sugar to taste	
1/4 tsp.	orange syrup	1 mL
	crushed ice	
2	thin orange slices	2
	cinnamon stick	

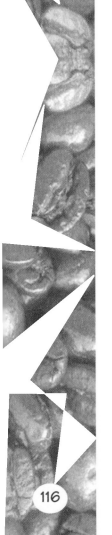

POUR   the coffee into a 16-oz. (500 mL) container.

ADD   the cinnamon, sugar and syrup to the cold coffee.

SERVE   in 2 glasses over crushed ice.

GARNISH each serving with an orange slice and a cinnamon stick for stirring.

Serves: 2

COFFEE IS A FLEETING MOMENT AND A FRAGRANCE.

-Claudia Roden, *Coffee — a Connoisseur's Companion*

Tropical Iced Coffee Cocktail

Keep your cool during hot summer days with this one!

1 cup	cold Espresso (or cold strong coffee)	250 mL
1/4 cup	milk (or cream)	60 mL
1/4 tsp.	rum flavoring (or 1 oz./30 mL light rum)	1 mL
	cracked ice	
	ice-cold sparkling mineral water	
	sugar syrup (see page 151)	

COMBINE the coffee, milk and rum flavoring and chill thoroughly.
POUR over cracked ice in a tall chilled glass.
ADD ice-cold sparkling mineral water as desired.
SWEETEN with sugar syrup as desired.
STIR gently and serve.

Serves: 1

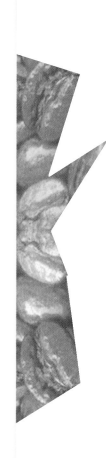

"MAZAGRAN", THE ORIGINAL ICED COFFEE WAS NAMED AFTER AN ALGERIAN FORTRESS. FRENCH COLONIAL TROOPS IN NORTHERN AFRICA CHILLED THE COFFEE TO COUNTER THE EXTREME TROPICAL HEAT.

Espresso Smoothie

A simple soul sweetener!

3 cups	cold Espresso	750 mL
	(or double-strength coffee)	
6 cups	ice	1.5 L
6	rock sugar swizzle sticks, (or sugar as needed)	6
6	lemon wedges	6

PLACE the Espresso and ice in a blender and blend until smooth.

ADD a swizzle stick, or desired sugar, to each of 6, 6-oz. (170 mL) glasses.

DIVIDE the Espresso/ice mixture evenly among 6 glasses.

SERVE with lemon wedges.

Serves: 6

IN POLITICS AS IT IS WITH COFFEE, THE ARGUMENTS FOR BOTH SIDES CAN BE PERSUASIVE. IT IS BEST TO FOLLOW YOUR OWN PALATE WHEN YOU CAST YOUR VOTE.

-ANONYMOUS

Cocoa-Mocha Coffee Shake

A chocolate coffee blend to shake up your daily grind!

2/3 cup	milk	150 mL
2/3 cup	cold sweetened Espresso	150 mL
2 scoops	coffee ice cream	2 scoops
2 scoops	chocolate ice cream	2 scoops
1 oz.	Kahlúa	30 mL
1 oz.	B-52 syrup (or crème de cacao)	30 mL
	grated chocolate for garnish	

BLEND   all ingredients, except grated chocolate, in a blender until creamy.

POUR   into 2 tall chilled glasses.

GARNISH with grated chocolate.

SIP   through fat straws.

Optional: For a non-alcoholic beverage, omit the Kahlúa.

Serves: 2

ONE LADY ACTUALLY SAID OUT LOUD IN A CORNER
COFFEEHOUSE - "YOU MEAN THIS ISN'T STARBUCKS?!"

Iced Irish Kah-fe-lúa

This cool one can certainly stand on its own.

3 oz.	Kahlúa (or B-52 syrup)	90 mL
1/2 tsp.	vanilla extract	2 mL
2 tbsp.	sugar	30 mL
6-8 oz.	cold Espresso (or strong coffee)	170-250 mL
	a few ice cubes	
	mounds of whipped cream	

STIR   Kahlúa, vanilla and sugar into the cold coffee.

FILL   two tall glasses with ice cubes and the cold coffee mixture.

TOP   with mounds of whipped cream.

Optional: coffee ice cubes may be substituted for ice cubes.

Serves: 2

Pictured opposite.

For an extra spike of Irish aroma:
> Use 1 oz. (30 mL) of Irish whiskey and 2 oz. (60 mL) of Kahlúa.

. . . BUT THERE'S BOOZE IN THE BLENDER AND SOON IT WILL RENDER THAT FROZEN CONCOCTION THAT HELPS ME HANG ON!

-Jimmy Buffet, Margaritaville

Iced Irish Kah-fe-lúa

DRINK
Coca-Cola

Cola Coffee

Cola-Coffee

This one offers a taste that beats coffee cold!

1 cup	strong coffee or Espresso	250 mL
4-6 oz.	Coke or Pepsi (your preference, of course)	113-170 mL

Optional: whipped cream and/or lemon

MIX   coffee and cola together in a tall glass, over ice.

Optional: Add whipped cream and/or lemon if desired.

Serves: 1

Pictured opposite.

Espresso Ice

So cool it rocks!

½ cup	cold Espresso (or strong coffee)	125 mL
3 cups	ice	750 mL
3	rock sugar swizzle sticks (or sugar as needed)	3
3	lemon wedges	3

BLEND   Espresso and ice in a blender until smooth.

ADD   a swizzle stick to each glass. Or, if using sugar, rub the rim of each glass with a lemon wedge, then dip it in sugar.

POUR   the Espresso Ice into 3 stemmed glasses and serve with lemon wedges and straws.

Serves: 3

FACT: IN 1996 PEPSI PRODUCED AN EXPERIMENTAL COFFEE SOFT DRINK CALLED "PEPSI KONA". COFFEE SODA CONCEPTS HAVE BEEN AROUND SINCE THE 1920'S!

Espresso Spritzer

Tired of the same old grind? Fizz it up with this one!

1 cup	cold Espresso	250 mL
	crushed ice	
	carbonated mineral water	

POUR   the Espresso over crushed ice or ice cubes
in a tall glass.

ADD   carbonated mineral water or soda water.

STIR   to blend.

Serves: 1

Variation: 1-2 oz. (30-60 mL) each of light cream or
chocolate syrup may be added if desired.

PRIOR TO COKE AND PEPSI, IT WAS VERY FASHIONABLE
IN ITALIAN BARS AND EUROPEAN CAFÉS TO ORDER
FLAVORED FIZZY BEVERAGES MADE OF COFFEE AND
SPARKLING WATER!

Frozen Mocha Mint Cappuccino

This frozen cappuccino treat is sure to cool you down, and lift your spirits at the same time!

8 oz.	cold Espresso (or strong coffee)	250 mL
2 cups	chocolate (or mocha) ice cream	500 mL
¼ cup	crème de menthe (or chocolate mint syrup)	60 mL
	whipped cream	
	very thin chocolate-mint wafers	

COMBINE Espresso, ice cream and crème de menthe in a blender.

BLEND on low speed until smooth.

SPOON into wine or sherbet glasses.

GARNISH each serving with a dollop of whipped cream and a chocolate-mint wafer.

Serves: 4

Q: WHAT'S A GUTLESS WONDER?
A: A DECAF NON-FAT LATTÉ!

Espresso Mocha Freeze

The sophisticated milkshake.

½ cup	hot fresh Espresso (or strong coffee)	125 mL
1²/₃ oz.	milk chocolate bar, broken up.	47 g
5-6	ice cubes	5-6
2 cups	vanilla ice cream	500 mL
	grated chocolate for garnish	

COMBINE Espresso and chocolate pieces in a blender.
allow the chocolate to soften.

ADD the ice to the coffee chocolate mixture and
blend until smooth.

ADD the ice cream and blend again.

POUR into 2 glasses.

SPRINKLE each serving with grated chocolate.

Serves: 2

BAR PATRONS GET INTOXICATED, GO HOME AND FALL
ASLEEP. COFFEEHOUSE PATRONS GET WIRED AND NEVER
LEAVE THE STORE!

Cappuccino Slush Cocktail

A sophisticated slushie!

1/4 cup	cold Espresso	60 mL
3/4 cup	milk (or ice cream)	175 mL
3/4 cup	ice cubes (or crushed ice)	175 mL
2 tsp.	sugar	10 mL
2 tsp.	chocolate syrup	10 mL

PLACE all ingredients in a blender and blend until smooth and thick.

SERVE immediately.

Serves: 2

Iced Amaretto Espresso Cocktail

There's nothing quite like this iced cocktail on a hot summer day.

	crushed ice	
2 oz.	cold Espresso	60 mL
1 oz.	amaretto (syrup or liqueur)	30 mL
1/2 cup	cold milk	125 mL

FILL a medium glass half full with crushed ice.

ADD the Espresso, then the amaretto and, finally, the cold milk.

STIR and serve immediately.

Serves: 1

EVEN IN THE ICY DEPTHS OF WINTER, RETAIL ICED CAPPUCCINO AND SLUSH DRINK SALES DECREASE BY ONLY 20% (APPROX.) FROM THE PEAK SELLING DAYS OF THE SUMMER HEAT!

Iced Orange Mochaccino

Take time to smell this mochaccino!

4-6 oz.	cold milk	113-170 mL
2-4	coffee ice cubes	2-4
2 oz.	cold Espresso	60 mL
1 tsp.	chocolate syrup	5 mL
2 oz.	caramel syrup	60 mL
2 oz.	orange juice	60 mL
1-2 oz.	orange liqueur (or orange-flavored syrup)	30-60 mL

POUR   the milk into a tall glass with the coffee ice cubes.

WHISK   the remaining ingredients until well blended.

POUR   the coffee/orange mixture into the milk.

STIR   and enjoy!

Serves: 1 tall

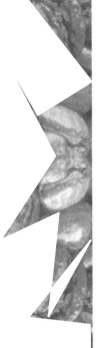

A RUDE ESPRESSO MAN SAYS YOU CAN CHOOSE CINNAMON OR CHOCOLATE OR GET LOST.

Brandy-Mocha Iced Café

Rock your world with this bold cold one!

12-15	coffee ice cubes (see page 130)	12-15 mL
1 cup	milk	250 mL
2 oz.	semisweet quality chocolate, (2 squares) melted	55 g
2 tbsp.	brandy (or brandy extract)	30 mL

COMBINE coffee ice cubes with milk, chocolate and brandy in a blender.

BLEND until frothy.

SERVE at once.

Serves: 2 small or 1 tall

THE WORD "MOCHA" ORIGINALLY REFERRED TO A SUPERIOR QUALITY OF COFFEE BEANS GROWN IN ARABIA AND SHIPPED FROM THE PORT OF MOCHA, IN YEMEN. TODAY, IT REFERS TO A DELICIOUS COMBINATION OF CHOCOLATE AND COFFEE.

Iced/Frozen Cappuccino

Start preparing this the day before for coffee ice cubes.

1 cup	Espresso (or strong coffee)	250 mL
6 oz.	cold milk	170 mL
2 tbsp.	sugar	30 mL
2 tbsp.	coffee syrup (see page 150)	30 mL

A day prior:
POUR the coffee into 2 ice cube trays and freeze*.

The next day:
PLACE coffee ice cubes, milk, sugar and coffee syrup in a blender.
BLEND until smooth.
POUR into chilled glasses.
SERVE immediately.

Serves: 2

Now you have the "secret" recipe for coffee ice cubes!

WHEN SOMEONE SAYS "HOW ARE YOU?", YOU CAN SAY, "GOOD TO THE LAST DROP!"

Festive Cappuccino Cocktails

. . . for the Holidays!

FROM CHRISTMAS CAPPOS TO LOVE POTION LATTES
- TURN FESTIVE OCCASIONS INTO ESPRESSO HOLIDAYS!

Cupid Cappuccino

For a special moment, especially Valentine's Day!

4 oz.	hot fresh Espresso	113 mL
1 oz.	chocolate syrup (or crème de cacao)	30 mL
1 oz.	crème de menthe (syrup or liqueur)	30 mL
1 oz.	amaretto (syrup or liqueur)	30 mL
	sugar, if desired	
8 oz.	hot foamed or frothed milk	250 mL
	whipped cream	

POUR   Espresso and syrups (or liqueurs) into 2 glass mugs. Add sugar if desired.

SCOOP   hot foamed milk onto the coffee in each mug.

TOP   with a dollop of whipped cream.

SERVE   with a kiss!

Serves: 2

Pictured on page 190.

ALL YOU NEED TO GET YOU IN THE MOOD IS . . . SOFT LIGHTS, ROMANTIC MUSIC AND A CUP OF "CUPID CAPPUCCINO"!

French Kiss Caffe Latte

Dedicated to my "French-Swiss" soulmate – Bobbie

½ oz.	vanilla syrup (or Bailey's or Tia Maria)	15 mL
½ oz.	caramel syrup (or Cointreau)	15 mL
4 oz.	hot steamed milk	113 mL
2 oz.	hot fresh Espresso	60 mL
	soft whipped cream	

POUR the syrups (or liqueurs) into 2 stemmed glass mugs.

ADD hot milk. DO NOT STIR.

ADD Espresso to the milk/syrup mixture.

TOP with a dollop of whipped cream; sprinkle with a kiss.

Serves: 2

Frozen Passion

Heat things up with this cold one!

2 oz.	cold Espresso	60 mL
½ oz.	chocolate syrup (or crème de cacao)	15 mL
½ oz.	hazelnut syrup (or Frangelico liqueur)	15 mL
½ cup	crushed ice	125 mL
1 cup	whipped cream (save 1 or 2 spoonfuls for topping)	250 mL
	cocoa powder	

BLEND the Espresso and syrups together in a blender.

ADD crushed ice and whipped cream to the blender.

BLEND the coffee, ice and whipped cream until thick and fluffy.

TOP with a dollop of whipped cream.

DUST with cocoa powder.

Serves: 1

AH! HOW SWEET COFFEE TASTES! LOVELIER THAN A THOUSAND KISSES, SWEETER THAN MUSCATEL WINE!

-J.S. BACH'S *COFFEE CANTANTA*, 1732

Love Potion Latte No. 9

"Una bella tazza di caffe":
Italian for a "beautiful cup of coffee".

1 oz.	almond syrup (or Grand Marnier)	30 mL
1 oz.	hazelnut syrup (or Frangelico)	30 mL
8 oz.	cold milk	250 mL
4 oz.	hot fresh Espresso (or strong coffee)	113 mL
	cocoa or cinnamon for garnish	

POUR syrups (or liqueurs) into 2, 12-oz. (340 mL) latte mugs.

STEAM the cold milk until it is almost double in volume.

POUR the hot Espresso into the syrups in the cups.

DOLLOP the frothed milk into the cups.

DUST with cocoa or cinnamon.

SERVE immediately.

Serves: 2

AS WITH MOST THINGS ITALIAN THERE IS A CERTAIN AURA OF ROMANCE ABOUT THESE DRINKS. ANYONE WHO'S HAD THE PLEASURE OF TICKLING AN UPPER LIP WITH THE CREAMY FOAM OF CAPPUCCINO KNOWS WHY.

-TIMOTHY JAMES CASTLE, THE PERFECT CUP, 1991

Irish Cream Latte

Perfect for St. Patrick's Day – but don't wait!

2 oz.	hot fresh Espresso	60 mL
1 oz.	Irish cream syrup (or preferred liqueur)	30 mL
6-8 oz.	steamed milk	170-250 mL
	whipped cream	
	Irish cream syrup (or liqueur) for drizzling	

COMBINE Espresso and syrup (or liqueur) in a 12-oz.
(340 mL) latte mug.

POUR steamed milk into coffee.

TOP with whipped cream.

DRIZZLE with syrup (or liqueurs).

Serves: 1

Frozen Leprechaun

Saint Patrick's Day

2 oz.	simple sugar syrup (see page 151)	60 mL
2-4 oz.	cold Espresso (or strong coffee)	60-113 mL
2 oz.	Irish whiskey *	60 mL
2 oz.	light cream	60 mL
2 cups	crushed ice	500 mL

COMBINE all ingredients in a blender and blend
until smooth.

POUR into a chilled tall glass.

Serves: 1 tall or 2 small

* Irish whiskey is optional

AN IRISHMAN IS NEVER DRUNK AS LONG AS HE CAN HOLD
ONTO A SINGLE BLADE OF GRASS WITHOUT FALLING OFF
THE FACE OF THE EARTH!

-ANONYMOUS

Thanksgiving Orange Latte

You'll be grateful for this one!

3/4 oz.	orange syrup (or Grand Marnier)	20 mL
1/4 oz.	amaretto (syrup or liqueur)	7 mL
2 oz.	hot fresh Espresso	60 mL
6-8 oz.	steamed half and half	170-250 mL
	whipped cream	
	decorative orange sprinkles	

POUR syrups (or liqueurs) into a 12-oz. (340 mL) latte or cappuccino mug.

ADD the Espresso to the syrups.

SCOOP frothy steamed half and half on top of the coffee and syrups.

TOP with whipped cream and decorative orange sprinkles, if desired.

Serves: 1

THANK YOU FOR OUR DAILY GRIND!

Hallowe'en Coffee Poem

Double, double, Espresso trouble . . .

THREE WITCHES PRODUCTIONS.

"Double, double, Espresso trouble,
Fire burn and cauldron bubble.
Finest grind of French Roast choose,
And with high-pressured steam infuse.
Foam of milk and cocoa dust,
Dash of sugar, if you must,
Cinnamon and nut of meg,
Morning paper on your leg.
For a charm of powerful trouble,
Like hell-broth Espresso trouble,
Fire burn and cauldron bubble."

-THE THREE WITCHES

THE WITCHES' BREW OF ESPRESSO COFFEE!

Christmas Cappuccino

Christmas à la crème.

4 oz.	eggnog	113 mL
2 oz.	hot fresh Espresso	60 mL
Optional:	1/2 oz. sambuca	15 mL
	1/2 oz. advocaat (egg liqueur)	15 mL

whipped cream
cinnamon or nutmeg

STEAM the eggnog until it is doubled in volume.
Pour eggnog into a tempered Christmas
glass or mug.

POUR Espresso gently down the side of the glass
into the steamed/frothed eggnog.

Optional: if using liqueurs, gently pour them into the
finished beverage.

SCOOP a dollop of whipped cream on top.

DUST with cinnamon or nutmeg.

SERVE immediately with small red and green
straws across the top of the cream, and/or
a cinnamon stick.

Serves: 1

Pictured opposite.

I JUST HAD SOME COFFEE THAT WAS GOOD ONLY FOR ITS "SEDIMENTAL" VALUE!

Christmas Cappuccino

Holly Jolly Espresso

Holly Jolly Espresso

This very festive cappuccino will surely warm your nose!

¹/₄ oz.	Tia Maria	7 mL
¹/₄ oz.	Bailey's	7 mL
¹/₄ oz.	Grand Marnier	7 mL
¹/₄ oz.	Frangelico	7 mL
¹/₄ oz.	dark crème de cacao	7 mL

(and don't forget the coffee!)

5-6 oz.	hot Espresso (or strong coffee)	145-170 mL
	cinnamon stick	
	whipped cream	

POUR all of the liqueurs into a tempered goblet or glass coffee mug.

FILL with hot coffee.

GARNISH with a cinnamon stick.

STIR once around, lifting up the liqueurs from the bottom of the mug or cup.

TOP with whipped cream.

Serves: 1

Pictured opposite.

. . . AND TO ALL A JOLLY GOOD NIGHT!

-SUSAN ZIMMER

Eggnog-a-ccino

An "egg-citing" holiday Espresso!

4	egg yolks	4
2 tsp.	sugar	10 mL
1/2 cup	hot fresh Espresso (or strong coffee)	125 mL
2 oz.	Bailey's (or coffee cream liqueur)	60 mL
dash	nutmeg	dash
1/4 tsp.	grated lemon peel	1 mL
	whipped cream	
	cocoa powder	
	grated lemon peel	

BEAT egg yolks with sugar in a bowl until smooth.

PLACE egg yolk/sugar mixture into a double boiler and, while stirring, gently bring temperature to about 110°F (45°C).

WHISK yolks with a hand mixer while adding the coffee, liqueur, nutmeg and lemon peel. Continue whisking until mixture becomes creamy.

DECORATE with whipped cream, cocoa powder and grated lemon peel.

Serves: 4

THE ITALIANS KNOW THAT EVERYTHING IN THEIR COUNTRY IS . . . IMBUED WITH THEIR SPIRIT. THEY ARE ALL WORKS OF ART, THE "GREAT ART OF BEING HAPPY AND MAKING OTHER PEOPLE HAPPY . . ."

-LUIGI BARZINI. *THE ITALIANS*

Candy Cane Latte

This drink will spread Christmas cheer.

3/4 oz.	cherry syrup (or Kirschwasser liqueur)	20 mL
1/4 oz.	crème de menthe (syrup or liqueur)	7 mL
2 oz.	hot fresh Espresso	30 mL
4-6 oz.	steamed milk	113-170 mL
	whipped cream	
	small candy canes	

POUR the syrups (or liqueurs) and Espresso into a 12-oz. (340 mL) latte mug.

ADD steamed milk.

TOP with whipped cream.

GARNISH with small candy canes hanging off the rim of the mug.

Serves: 1

DIVINA FLOR, SERVED SANTIAGO NASAR WITH A MUG OF COUNTRY COFFEE, LACED WITH SUGAR-CANE ALCOHOL, JUST AS SHE DID EVERY MONDAY, TO HELP HIM GET OVER THE PREVIOUS NIGHT'S FATIGUE.

-GABRIEL GARCIA MÁRQUEZ, CHRONICLE OF A DEATH FORETOLD

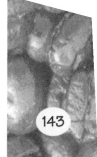

Orange Yule Delight Latte

"Yule" shine with delight as you serve this one!

4 oz.	light cream or milk	113 mL
2 oz.	hot fresh Espresso	60 mL
3/4 oz.	orange syrup (or Grand Marnier liqueur)	20 mL
1/4 oz.	amaretto (syrup or liqueur)	7 mL
	whipped cream	

STEAM   light cream or milk until hot and frothy (double in volume).

POUR   into a tempered mug.

POUR   hot Espresso and syrups (or liqueurs) into the frothy cream.

TOP   with whipped cream.

Serves: 1

DRINK PLENTY OF IT, IN ITS FLAVOR WORRIES DISAPPEAR - AND ITS FIRE BURNS AWAY THE DARK THOUGHTS OF EVERYDAY LIFE!

-HADJIBUN, ARABIAN JURIST

Festive Espresso Eggnog

Make it once and they'll want you to make it every year!

1 oz.	chocolate syrup or rum	30 mL
2 oz.	hot fresh Espresso	60 mL
4-6 oz.	steamed eggnog	113-170 mL
	cocoa powder or nutmeg	

COMBINE chocolate syrup and Espresso in a 12-oz.
(340 mL) Christmas mug. Stir until blended.

FILL the cup with steamed eggnog.

DUST with cocoa powder or nutmeg.

Serves: 1

YOU ARE THE ONE DIVINE COFFEE WHOSE SWEET LIQUOR,
WITHOUT ALTERING THE MIND, CAN MAKE THE HEART
BLOOM.

-ABBÉ DELILLE (1738-1813), FRENCH POET

Happy Holiday Coffee Punch

A yummy crowd pleaser.

1 cup	whipping cream	250 mL
1/4 tsp.	salt	1 mL
1/2 cup	sugar	125 mL
1/4 tsp.	almond extract	1 mL
1/2 tsp.	vanilla	2 mL
1 quart	cold strong coffee or Espresso	1 L
	(leftover works well!)	
1 quart	vanilla ice cream	1 L
1 quart	chocolate ice cream	1 L
1/2 tsp.	nutmeg	2 mL
1/4 tsp.	cinnamon	1 mL

WHIP the whipping cream in a separate bowl, slowly adding the salt, sugar, almond extract and vanilla.

POUR the chilled coffee into a punch bowl.

ADD walnut-size chunks of the vanilla and chocolate ice creams

FOLD the whipped cream into the punch.

SPRINKLE with nutmeg and cinnamon.

Serves: 35

AMONGST THE NUMEROUS LUXURIES OF THE TABLE . . .
COFFEE MAY BE CONSIDERED AS ONE OF THE MOST
VALUABLE . . . THE PLEASING FLOW OF SPIRITS WHICH IT
OCCASIONS.

-SIR BENJAMIN THOMPSON, COUNT RUMFORD (1753-1814)

Coffee Syrup Recipes 'n' Tips

As passionate cappuccino lovers know,
creating flavor is an art . . . not a show!
Sinfully decadent are these drinks;
a latte laced with syrup . . . what do you think?

Endless flow of flavor fusions,
adds excitement to the coffee confusion!
Syrups are the paints for flavor flair,
inspiring new recipes . . . take the dare!

-Susan M. Zimmer

There is a recipe movement out there! Gourmet flavored syrups expose us to new coffee beverage experiences, and allow for more complex and creative uses of flavors. Almost any prepared flavored syrup can be added to coffees, Espressos, lattes, steamers and cappuccinos. Flavored syrups can also be added to chocolate or white chocolate syrups, then mixed with Espresso to make creamy mocha coffees! Syrups provide elegant texture and extra smoothness to your coffee beverages.

When ordinary coffee just won't do, become your own barista. Don't be afraid to explore new flavor delights. Challenge syrups to help you create extraordinary Espresso-based beverages.

Discover new palate possibilities with these suggested popular flavors for hot or cold coffee drinks.

LIST OF SUITABLE SENSATIONAL SYRUPS:

Vanilla, hazelnut, almond, mocha (Bavarian chocolate) Irish cream, amaretto, B-52, white chocolate, caramel cream, Frangelico (hazelnut/vanilla), raspberry, English toffee.

Some fruit flavors also work well, e.g., orange and raspberry.

Stretch your imagination, not to mention your coffee menu, with the following tips and recipes to use in coffees, Espressos, Italian sodas, colas, shakes and smoothies (don't forget desserts, cola-based beverages and ice creams, too!).

FLAVORED SYRUP TIPS

- When adding flavored syrups to coffee beverages, syrups should be combined with HOT Espresso, or coffee and then stirred. This thoroughly blends the two flavors together. If you are making a milk-based coffee beverage, then milk may be added to flavored Espresso and stirred again. These taste great over crushed/cubed ice as COLD drinks, too!

- Another option for HOT specialty flavored coffee is to first steam the milk with the chosen syrups and then allow it to sit while preparing the hot Espresso. Steam infuses the syrup and milk with extra flavor richness.

- Syrups will eliminate the need for sugar and other sweeteners. Don't add too much syrup because you want to enjoy the original rich coffee flavor. Remember, 2 teaspoons (10 mL) of syrup are equivalent to about 1 teaspoon (5 mL) of sugar, but will deliver two to three times as much flavor enhancement!

- *Spirited Syrups:* Your own favorite liqueur (or Schnaps) can be made by combining syrups with vodka in a one to one ratio: 1 ounce (30 mL) of syrup with 1 ounce (30 mL) of vodka. For example, mix hazelnut and/or crème de menthe syrups with vodka to make liqueurs and serve with coffees and desserts. Mix dark chocolate syrup with vodka, then add steamed milk and Espresso for a "Mud slide" Mocha Café!

- *Iced Coffee Drink varieties* are quick and easy when using syrups. For each 12-ounce (340 mL) drink, add 1 ounce (30 mL) of your favorite syrup to a glass or cup. Add 1 to 2 ounces (30 to 60 mL) of Espresso or strong coffee, then ice cubes; stir well and fill with ice-cold milk. Top with whipped cream, if desired. Garnish with a cherry, chocolate shavings or cinnamon.

- *General measurement guidelines for individual 5 to 6-ounce (145 to 170 mL) cappuccinos, lattes or cafés au lait:* add 1 to 2 teaspoons (5 to 10 mL) of flavored syrups (or to preferred taste). For each 1$^1/2$ ounce (45 mL) of Espresso add 1 teaspoon (5 mL) of flavored syrup, or to preferred taste.

- *Simple hot Café Mochas* can be made be adding 2 tablespoons (30 mL) of dark (or white) chocolate syrup to Espresso and steamed milk. For an *Iced Café Mocha* version, simply do the same as for the "hot" and serve in a tall glass filled with ice, or even better – coffee ice cubes!

- *Smoothies and shakes:* By mixing syrups and other ingredients in a blender you can experience endless summer sipping combinations! *A Mocha Café Milkshake,* for example, can be made by mixing 2$^1/2$ cups (625 mL) vanilla ice cream, 2 ounces (60 mL) of Espresso, 1 ounce (30 mL) of chocolate syrup in a blender.

- For *Cappuccino Fruit Cocktail* lovers combine 1$^3/4$ cups (425 mL) ice, $^1/4$ cup (60 mL) blackberries, 2 ounces (60 mL) raspberry syrup, 1 to 2 ounces (30 to 60 mL) Espresso coffee. Mix in blender until smooth.

- *Simple Sugar Syrup, see recipe on page 151, is recommended when sweetening iced or cold coffee drinks. It dissolves better than granulated sugar in cold liquids.*

Coffee Syrup

This versatile syrup is perfect for making iced coffees. It is also great for desserts and over ice cream, too!

2 cups	hot fresh Espresso (or strong coffee)	500 mL
1¹/₃ cups	sugar	325 mL
1	vanilla bean, split lengthwise	1
¹/₃ cup	dark roast coffee beans (slightly cracked)	75 mL
¹/₈ tsp.	salt	0.5 mL

COMBINE the coffee, sugar, vanilla bean, coffee beans and salt in a medium saucepan.

COOK over low heat, stirring frequently, until sugar is dissolved.

BOIL over medium-high heat and cook, without stirring, for about 4 minutes, or until thick and syrupy.

REMOVE the saucepan from the heat and cool completely.

STRAIN the coffee mixture through a fine sieve into a small bowl.

DISCARD the coffee beans and, if desired, set the vanilla bean aside for another use.*

COVER the syrup with plastic wrap and chill until ready to use.

Yield: about 1 cup (250 mL)

VANILLA SUGAR TIP

* Wash and dry the vanilla bean, then push it into the middle of a 6-cup (1.5 L) container filled with granulated sugar. Set aside, covered, for 2 weeks. This "vanilla sugar", with its delicate vanilla aroma and flavor, can now be used for baking or sweetening just about anything.

Simple Sugar Syrup

Simply the best way to sweeten iced coffee drinks!

Equal quantities of sugar and water

SIMMER sugar and water in a saucepan for about 5 minutes, until sugar is totally dissolved.

COOL thoroughly.

STORE in a covered jar in the refrigerator.

Espresso Syrup

Another handy flavoring to have in the kitchen, it is also easy to prepare. This rich syrup can be used as a sweet flavoring in iced coffees (or on waffles, pancakes or ice cream too!).

³/₄ cup	white granulated sugar (or vanilla sugar, see page 155)	175 mL
¹/₄ cup	water	60 mL
4 oz.	hot fresh Espresso (or strong coffee)	113 mL

COMBINE the sugar and water in a small saucepan and bring to a boil. Lower the heat and let simmer for 5 minutes.

REMOVE from the heat and let cool for 1 minute.

STIR in the Espresso.

ALLOW the syrup to sit at least 30 minutes before using.

STORE the syrup in a sealed jar in the refrigerator. It will keep for several weeks (if you don't tell anyone it's there!).

Yield: 1 cup (250 mL)

Optional: For a spiced variation, try stirring in 2 tsp. (10 mL) grated orange peel and 1 tsp. (5 mL) cinnamon with the Espresso.

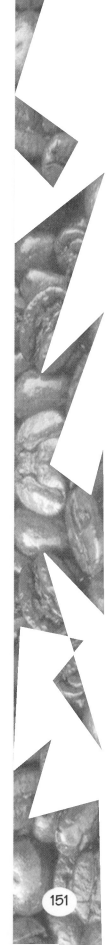

151

Chocolate Syrup

Mmmmm . . . very chocolate-y

1½ cups	granulated sugar	375 mL
1 cup	sifted unsweetened Dutch cocoa powder	250 mL
few grains	salt	few grains
1 cup	water	250 mL
2 tsp.	vanilla	10 mL

COMBINE the sugar, cocoa powder and salt in a saucepan.

WHISK thoroughly.

ADD water gradually to the cocoa, stirring (not beating) with a whisk to blend thoroughly.

PLACE over medium heat, stirring frequently with the whisk until mixture comes to a boil. A layer of foam may form on top of the syrup.

BOIL for 3 minutes, stirring at all times with the whisk. Reduce the heat if the syrup threatens to boil over.

REMOVE from heat; pour into a heatproof liquid measuring cup (3 cup/750 mL capacity).

COOL briefly, then chill, uncovered, in the refrigerator until completely cold.

STRAIN through a fine strainer into a 2½ cup (625 mL) container.

STIR in vanilla.

STORE covered, in the refrigerator.

Yield: 1¾ cups (425 mL)

Whipped Cream Recipes 'n' Tips

- To achieve the best results and full volume, chill the bowl and beaters in advance. Make sure that the cream (35% milk fat) is very cold before it is whipped.

- If using an electric beater, run on medium speed until the cream begins to thicken. Lower the speed and watch carefully. DO NOT OVERBEAT. (Like egg whites, cream can be overbeaten. Overbeaten cream begins to look granular and eventually lumps will form. If whipping continues, the cream will turn into butter.)

- "Soft peaks" will begin to form, whether whipping is done by hand-whisking or with a mixing machine at a moderate speed. The "soft peaks" stage is when mounds can be dropped from the whisk or beaters. This is the correct time to add sugar, vanilla sugar or other flavoring ingredients.

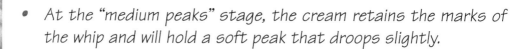

- At the "medium peaks" stage, the cream retains the marks of the whip and will hold a soft peak that droops slightly.

- At the "stiff peaks" stage, the cream forms distinct mounds that hold their shape.

- Keeping cream stiff for longer periods of time, can be achieved by adding Oetker's Whip it (stabilizer), or use icing (confectioner's) sugar – it contains about 3 percent cornstarch which helps stabilize the whipped cream.

- Entertaining for an evening? In order to have whipped cream ready ahead of time for the Cappuccino Cocktail dessert drinks, beat the cream and pipe it through a pastry tube fitted with a decorative tip. Squeeze dollops onto a cookie sheet lined with foil. Freeze these individual dollops uncovered, then wrap them in foil and place in the freezer for convenient use. They should be used within two months.

- Whipped cream can be prepared up to 4 hours ahead. Cover and chill until ready to use.

- Quick, convenient and much too easy! Using a whipped cream siphon-dispensing machine is the easiest way to make fluffy, superior whipped cream without the use of a whisk or beater. You simply pour 2 cups (500 mL) or so of 35% MF cream into the dispensing can, attach a gas cartridge to the dispensing top, shake a few times and depress the trigger. The advantage to this method, is that unused cream can be safely stored up to two weeks by placing the entire container in the fridge. No bowls, utensils or countertops have to be cleaned. Simply rinse the container. These fantastic machines are available at most department or kitchen specialty stores.

- Add your favorite flavor to whipped cream or whipped topping by adding 1 to 2 tbsp. (15 to 30 mL) of your favorite syrup to 2 cups (500 mL) of whipping cream. Beat until medium or stiff peaks form. Some suggested flavors are: B-52, amaretto, caramel cream, mocha and English toffee.

Vanilla Whipped Cream

This one's a keeper! A European traditional
recipe I learned from Tante Maria!

2 cups	chilled whipping cream (35% MF) (1 pint)	500 mL
3 tbsp.	vanilla sugar*	45 mL

WHIP   the cream on medium speed with an electric
mixer until soft peaks form.

ADD   vanilla sugar, 1 tbsp. (15 mL) at at time.
DO NOT OVERBEAT.

SERVE   immediately or store in refrigerator up to
4 hours before serving.

VANILLA SUGAR* TIPS

- Prepared vanilla sugar packets may be found at most
  grocery outlets in the baking section.

- However, you can make your own vanilla sugar by
  purchasing 1 or 2 vanilla beans. (They are long, thin, dark
  pods and pleasantly aromatic.)
  In a large tin or glass container, which has a tight cover,
  insert 1 long vanilla bean into the middle of 8 cups (2 L) of
  white granulated sugar. Place a tight-fitting lid on the
  container and allow it to sit for a minimum of 2 weeks.
  All the wonderful aromas marry with the sugar. Great for
  baking or use instead of regular sugar and vanilla extract.

- The vanilla beans may be reused for up to 6 months to
  make more vanilla sugar.

Espresso Whipped Cream

An "over-the-top" Espresso indulgence!

1 cup	chilled whipping cream	250 mL
3 tbsp.	golden brown sugar	45 mL
1 tsp.	vanilla extract	5 mL
1 tsp.	instant Espresso powder	5 mL

WHIP all ingredients in medium-sized, chilled bowl until soft peaks form.

SERVE immediately or store in refrigerator until needed.

Yield: about 2 cups (500 mL)

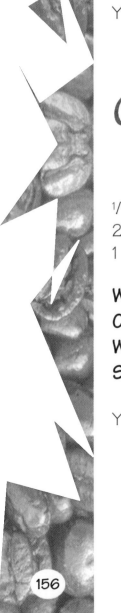

Coffee Whipped Cream

This is wonderful on any Cappuccino Cocktail speciality coffee recipe.

½ cup	chilled whipping cream	125 mL
2 tbsp.	sugar	30 mL
1 tbsp.	instant coffee	15 mL

WHIP the cream with the sugar and instant coffee.

CHILL at least 3 hours.

WHIP again until peaks form.

SERVE immediately.

Yield: about 1 cup (250 mL)

Cinnamon Whipped Cream

Simply great for all coffee and cinnamon lovers!

1 cup	whipping cream	250 mL
3 tbsp.	icing (confectioner's) sugar	45 mL
1 tsp.	ground cinnamon	5 mL

COMBINE all the ingredients in a mixing bowl.

WHIP until soft peaks form.

CHILL until ready to serve.

Yield: approximately 2 cups (500 mL)

Kahlúa Whipped Cream

Absolutely fabulous on a cappuccino cocktail!

1 cup	whipping cream	250 mL
1/2 cup	sifted icing (confectioner's) sugar	125 mL
3 tbsp.	Kahlúa (or Kahlúa syrup)	45 mL

WHIP whipping cream in a mixing bowl until foamy.

GRADUALLY ADD sifted icing sugar.

WHIP until soft peaks form.

FOLD in Kahlúa (or syrup).

COVER and chill until ready to serve.

Yield: 2 cups (500 mL)

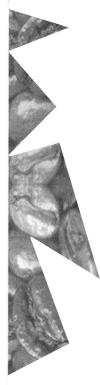

Chocolate Whipped Cream

A chocolate lover's topping for mochaccinos, or for a plain cup of joe.

1 cup	whipping cream	250 mL
3 tbsp.	icing sugar	45 mL
2 tbsp.	cocoa powder	30 mL
1/2 tsp.	crème de cacao	2 mL

WHIP the cream in a chilled bowl, using an electric mixer, until soft peaks form.

FOLD in dry ingredients 1 tbsp. (15 mL) at a time.

FOLD in the crème de cacao.

CHILL for 30 minutes before using.

Yield: 2 to 2 1/2 cups (500 to 625 mL)

Soy Whipped Cream

The alternative whipped cream!

1/4 cup	soy milk	60 mL
1/2 cup	vegetable oil	125 mL
1 tbsp.	maple syrup	15 mL
1/2 tsp.	vanilla extract	2 mL

PLACE soy milk and 1/4 cup (60 mL) of the oil in a blender.

BLEND at highest speed and slowly drizzle in remaining 1/4 cup (60 mL) of oil.

BLEND in syrup and vanilla, adding a little more oil if necessary, to thicken.

SERVE immediately to top coffee beverages or your favorite baking recipes.

COFFEE: Rich in History

"IN EUROPE, THE MOST OBSTREPEROUS NATIONS ARE
THOSE MOST ADDICTED TO COFFEE.
WE RIGHTLY SPEAK OF A 'STORM IN A TEACUP' AS THE
TINIEST DISTURBANCE IN THE WORLD,
BUT OUT OF A COFFEE-CUP COME HURRICANES."
-ROBERT LYND

PART 1
THE KARMA OF COFFEE

Robert Lynd's quote, "... out of a coffee-cup come hurricanes ...", refers to coffee's capacity to create world economic pressures and its tremendous power and influence. This globe-trotting coffee bean is an ancient commodity, which has passionately traveled the world, migrating from country to country, inspiring and influencing lifestyles along the way. Since its humble origins in AD 575, more than a millennium ago, it has inspired storms of violence, piracy, smugglers, warriors, pilgrims and poets. It has continuously created dramatic disturbances and weathered turbulent times around the world, affecting many cultures and countries. As it did then, so it does today. Throughout time, the continuum of coffee consumption has become a global force of commerce – an intense cyclone of trading commodities.

Coffee and commerce have brewed up hurricanes of political opinion, from powerful governments and nations to trading cartels, over the ages. The winds of its aroma have influenced and been influenced by culture, health claims, religious fanatacism and public opinions across a long line of humanity. Coffee's karmic energy still influences events today, as it did in the old world.

Once upon a time I heard Sir Elton John sing "... you can make history young ...", as I was sipping my favorite steamy brew. I believe that the history of coffee consciousness is reborn again, time after time. Coffee is history itself! This globe-trotter has "bean" there, done that, many times! The pure essence and evolution of coffee could very well be a powerful physical space-time link to events over the ages, from the origins of human experience to the present moment.

COFFEE ORIGINS – LEGENDS AND LORE

AD 575 Ethiopia (where coffee still grows wild today) was the first known birthplace of coffee. Coffee was first eaten by Ethiopian tribes as a solid energy food. The beans from the red berry tree were crushed, combined with animal fat, then chewed as a source of energy (perhaps the world's first energy bar!).

Arabian traders were the first to "export" coffee and Ethiopian slaves to Yemen, the southern tip of the Arabian peninsula.

The Persians smuggled coffee from Ethiopia across the Red Sea to Yemen.

Legend has it, that coffee was discovered when Khaldi, a young Ethiopian goat herder noticed his goats' eccentric behavior after eating the red berries of a coffee bush. He began to eat them as well. The abbot from a nearby monastery witnessed Khaldi's bursts of energy and experimented with the beans in a beverage form. They were brewed with cold water into a form of wine, and served to the monks to help them stay awake during long prayer periods.

News of the berry drink spread rapidly throughout all the monasteries of the kingdom. Coffee, as it was known then, was quickly embraced by various Muslim sects for devotional purposes and enlightenment.

875   Arabian philosopher Rhazes confirmed, in the earliest known written remarks on coffee, that Ethiopia was the birthplace of the coffea arabica.

1000   Arabian physician and philosopher Avicenna of Bukhara was the first to describe the medicinal properties of coffee:
"It fortifies the members, it cleans the skin, and dries up the humidities that are under it, and gives an excellent smell to all the body."

1200   The Arabs, jealous of their discovery, blocked all transport of green coffee beans (which could germinate) from their country for years. This was the Arabs' attempt to control the commerce of coffee.

1258   Legend has it Sheik Hadji Omar, a religious physician from the city of Mocha in Yemen, used the red coffee berries as a remarkable stimulating thick brew to treat his patients. His patients were invigorated by this new medicine.

1400   Cheng Ho, a Chinese Admiral, exported the concept of an infused hot beverage to the Middle East.

1500   Mocha, a port in Yemen on the Red Sea, as well as Jidda, a port of Mecca, became the main ports for potential coffee traders.

The passion for coffee drinking continued to grow. Wherever people tasted coffee, they wanted it. The drink from the beloved berries came to be considered as important as bread and water.

Have they no water? Let them drink coffee!
-MARIE ANTOINETTE (1755-1793), QUEEN OF FRANCE

In fact, a Turkish law was passed during this period, making it grounds for divorce, if a husband should refuse to accept "kahve" (the Turkish word giving rise to the English word "coffee") from his wife!

1554   Drinking coffee became so popular that drinkers clustered in special areas to drink it. These areas became known as *"schools of wisdom"*, where intellectual and scholastic men would gather to discuss poetry, politics and other cultural subjects. The *world's first coffee houses originated in Constantinople* (Istanbul), Turkey.

Coffee is the milk of thinkers, and of chess players.
-ARABIC SAYING, CIRCA 1500

In Mecca and Cairo, coffee faced *religious intolerance*, since pious Muslims protested that the coffee houses were too full and the mosques were too empty.

1570   Coffee, coupled with its soulmate tobacco, made its first appearance in Venice. A doctor brought sacks of coffee beans back from a visit to Egypt. *Venice soon became the center of coffee trade with the East.*

1575   Religious fanatics claimed that coffee was an invention of Satan. Religious authorities in Constantinople ordered coffee houses to close their doors.

1587   The passion for coffee inspired the frequent patrons of the popular coffee houses known as *"schools of the cultured"*. One of the earliest poems referring to the romance around this *brown gold* beverage was recorded:

Where coffee is served, there is grace and splendor and friendship and happiness.
-SHEIKH ANSARI DJERZERI HANBALL ABD-AL-KADIR (1587)

1590   Coffee remained *a controlled monopoly of the Arab world*. Its cultivation secrets were jealously guarded. Foreigners were forbidden from visiting coffee farms, and the treasured beans could be exported only after heating or boiling, to destroy their germinating potential.

PART 2
COFFEE RULES . . . THE "OLD" WORLD

By the turn of the seventeenth century, coffee's karmic energy had already been both sanctified and damned as Satan's brew; praised by kings and prohibited by sultans. Coffee was now highly controversial in areas of religion, politics, arts, culture and cuisine. Enterprising traders, nomads and spies continued to passionately pursue and smuggle the precious red berry bean to capitalize on the "black elixir" it could produce. Coffee was highly sought after, because of public demand and the commerce it could command.

Coffee had come into the possession of enough different interest groups that its spread around the world had now become inevitable. Where issues of power and money developed between people, politics and nations, the powerful coffee bean was often in the eye of the storm, behind all the economic and political turbulence.

COFFEE'S CONQUEST CONTINUES

1600   A Moslem pilgrim from India, Baba Budan, quickly recognized the growing demand for coffee while visiting the Middle East. He smuggled the first germinable seeds from Mecca to southern India.

1616   Enterprising Dutch spies smuggled coffee plants from Mocha in Yemen to Holland. The Dutch devotion to the drink increased over the next few decades.
        The great coffee empire encompassed the borders of Persia, down to Arabia and over to Vienna.
        Visitors to this area recorded what they saw.

> They sit around sipping a drink which imitates that in the Stygian lake, black, thick and bitter.
>
> –SIR THOMAS HERBERT, DESCRIPTION OF PERSIAN COFFEE HOUSES (1620)

1623   Istanbul's governor closed the coffee houses because of speeches against the government. The Turks, however, needed their coffee and drank it secretly. If they were caught punishment was severe. For the first drink of coffee, the offender was beaten with a stick. For the second, he was sewn in a leather bag and dumped into the sea.

1645   Venice, Italy opened its first coffee house. Religious intolerance and prejudice briefly suppressed coffee's popularity, as they had done in the Middle East in 1575.

        The Catholic Church looked upon coffee as a drink from the devil. Pope Clement VIII, who decided to taste the beverage himself, also fell under the spell of the intoxicating beverage.

Why, this Satan's drink is so delicious, it would be a pity to let the infidels have exclusive use of it. We shall fool Satan by baptizing it and making it a truly Christian beverage.

-POPE CLEMENT VIII (1645)

1650   A Turkish entrepreneur opened the first English coffee house in Oxford, England, where the royal society was formed. These meeting places became England's first social clubs!

Lloyds of London also evolved from a coffee house, one that catered mainly to merchants and seafarers. Some patrons caught up on the latest shipping news,

1658   The first serious coffee cultivation took place in Ceylon (Sri Lanka), a Dutch-controlled colony.

1659   Venetian merchants brought coffee to Marseilles. A few years later, other merchants brought in the first commercial shipment from Egypt.

1660   Coffee was proclaimed as having medicinal qualities, and the Puritans at the time also thought coffee was a remedy to the widespread problem of public drunkenness.

. . . fewer drunken songs o'night time, fewer nobles lying in the gutter . . . Coffee the sobering beverage, a mighty nutriment of the brain, unlike spirituous Liquors, increases purity and clarity; coffee, which clears the imagination . . .

-JULES MICHELET, FRENCH HISTORIAN (1798-1874)

1665   A locksmith in London invented the first coffee mill.

1669   A Turkish ambassador influenced Paris society – coffee drinking is highly fashionable – thus its popularity with Paris's capitalistic bourgeoisie. Everything Turkish came into vogue.

A Turkish ambassador in Paris made the beverage highly fashionable . . . the brilliant porcelain cups, in which it was poured; the napkins fringed with gold, and the Turkish slaves on their knees presenting it to the ladies, seated on cushions, turned the heads of the Parisian dames. This elegant introduction made the exotic beverage a subject of conversation.

-ISAAC D'ISRAELI, PARIS (1670)

1670   In America's New Amsterdam (New York) the first license to sell coffee was issued.

The Dutch continued to cultivate coffee in Sumatra, Bali, Timor, Celebs and Dutch Guiana.

The French planted coffee in their colonies in the Caribbean and South America, and later in their colonies in Africa.

The Portugese produced coffee in parts of Indonesia and Brazil.

Destructive forces, such as the slave trade and massive forest clearing, continued to spread throughout virgin foreign territories controlled by various European colonial powers. Coffee was now a powerful cash crop, and colonialism dictated where coffee was to be cultivated.

1674   Women were not allowed in England's coffee houses. This led to a published protest: "The Women's Petition Against Coffee", protesting their being left alone too much in the evenings. Men responded with their defense of coffee houses, "The Men's Answer To The Women's Petition Against Coffee".

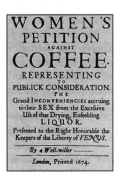

*Published protest of
The Women's Petition
and
The Men's Answer.*

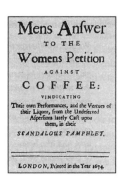

1675   *King Charles II finally reacted to this public discord between men and women, and proclaimed a decree to close down London's coffee houses. Coffee dealers protested, insisting that even the King was benefiting from the large revenues from the coffee trade.*
The Royal ruling was rescinded with provisions made for increased business taxes. Proprietors of the coffee houses were also forbidden freedom of speech.

1679   *Doctors in Marseilles became threatened by coffee usage and they attempted to discredit coffee by claiming it was harmful to one's health.*

1680   *Germany's first coffee house was opened in Hamburg. Slowly, coffee began to replace warm beer and flour soup at the breakfast tables in German homes!*

1683   *After the Turks were defeated in battle outside Vienna, Austria, they abandoned their supplies, camels and livestock. One of the exotic supplies left behind was coffee beans! A Polish man recognized them from his Middle Eastern travels and opened Vienna's first coffee house.*

1685   *Adding milk to coffee to create the first "café au laits" became popular when a French physician recommended this combination be used for medicinal purposes.*

1686   *An Italian opened the first real Parisian Café, Café de Procope, which still exists as a restaurant. Coffee drinking became fashionable and chic. This café attracted artists, authors, poets and actors. A new generation of artistic culture was born. Coffee was referred to as the intellectual's beverage.*

1696   *New York's first coffee house arrived, the King's Arms. Coffee houses expanded and became centers for social urban life. Coffee drinking fuelled social upheaval and political interaction.*

1697   *Dutch traders, ever anxious to explore, took coffee to Java (where it still grows today).*

1714   *Europe's first greenhouse, in Paris, the famous Jardin des Plantes, houses a noble 5' (1.5m) Java coffee tree. It was a gift to Louis XIV of France from the mayor of Amsterdam, Holland. From that single tree sprang billions of descendant arabica coffee trees (including those presently growing in Central and South America today)!*

| 1720 | The first coffee seedlings from the noble coffee tree in Paris, reached Martinique in the Caribbean, by way of a Dutch spy. |

| 1727 | A Brazilian, sent by royal authorities, obtained Brazils' first coffee seeds from the wife of the Governor of French Guiana. These golden seeds he brought back to Brazil are considered to have given birth to Brazil's current billion dollar coffee industry. |

| 1730 | The English brought coffee cultivation to Jamaica. Each year, 30,000 African slaves were imported to work the rapidly expanding coffee plantations. British colonials organized plantation systems in India, and set up the necessary processing and export facilities. |

| 1731 | Johann Sebastian Bach, a German composer and avid coffee drinker wrote "The Coffee Cantata". This sophisticated piece of music reflected the increasing paranoia about coffee addiction. |

How sweet coffee tastes! Livelier than a thousand kisses. Sweeter than muscatel wine. Oh, I must have my coffee! The only man who pleases me is the man who presents me with coffee.

-JOHANN SEBASTIAN BACH, "THE COFFEE CANTATA #211" (1732)

| 1737 | New York's Merchant Coffee House opened its doors, becoming an important center for the Chamber of Commerce. It is believed to be the first establishment to register and record the arrival of new citizens coming to the "New America". |

| 1770 | In the New World, coffee played second fiddle to tea – until political tensions grew over unfair taxation laws upon British colonies by King George III. The Merchant Coffee House, in Boston, became the arena for the planned boycott of imported English goods, the Boston Tea Party. Local citizens boarded English ships in Boston harbor and threw the British tea cargo overboard, crowning coffee as the "King of the American breakfast table". |

1775 In the American West, coffee had become a necessity. It was so important to pioneers and cowboys that they felt they couldn't do without it. During the Mexican-American and Civil wars, coffee was a vital part of the rations. The great American drink had to be strong enough to walk on its own! If it was too weak Mark Twain had something to say about it, comparing it to the stronger European coffee!

The average American's simplest . . . breakfast consists of coffee and beefsteak . . . (European coffee resembles the real thing like hypocrisy resembles holiness). It is a feeble, characterless, uninspiring sort of stuff. Not like the rich beverage of home, with its clotted layer of yellow cream on top of it.

-MARK TWAIN, AMERICAN WRITER AND HUMORIST (1835-1910)

1777 King Frederick the Great of Prussia realized the huge amounts of money flowing to foreign coffee merchants and sought to ban coffee. He issued a manifesto denouncing coffee in favor of the national drink – beer! He also favored chicory, a domestic substitute.

Have they no grounds? Let them drink chicory, but I would rather suffer with coffee, than be senseless.

-NAPOLEON BONAPARTE (1769-1821)

1781 Due to public demand, coffee defiantly fought to stay! The Prussian authorities placed a royal monopoly on the drink and coffee supplies had to be purchased from the government, which increased the King's income substantially! Coffee roasting licenses were not available to commoners.
The King had turned coffee into a drink of the nobility. Since he decided drinking coffee was a luxury for him, he boiled up his own coffee – not with water, but with champagne!

1784 In Cologne, Germany, another ban on coffee was issued among the lower classes, making large coffee quantities available only to the wealthy.

1786   The anti-coffee bans in Europe led to black markets, political laws, economic unrest and social upheaval. The people became frustrated without coffee.

Thank God, in the next world there will be no coffee.
For there is nothing more hellish than waiting for coffee
when it hasn't yet arrived!
-IMMANUEL KANT, GERMAN PHILOSOPHER (1724-1804)

1790   French Haiti became the world's largest coffee exporter, supplying half of the world's coffee, cultivated by nearly half a million slaves.

1793   The entire slave population in Haiti revolted and destroyed entire islands of coffee plantations and estates, causing French Haiti to lose its pre-eminent world production status.

1800   Brazil exported its first coffee shipment.

1801   A handbill was published in Milan, in which physicians held coffee in high esteem, calling it a "cure-all". It was the first advertisement for coffee, which was valued for its healing properties and as a restorative infusion.

        Coffee houses turned into real political arenas; newspapers were founded in coffee houses.

        Writers, politicians, great speakers and thinkers would gather in these "thinking institutions" to share their common interests and thoughts about democracy and freedom. Emotions were high and the resulting unrest often lead to revolutions.

Coffee surely makes the politician wise,
and see through all things with his eyes half-shut!
-ALEXANDER POPE, ENGLISH POET (1688-1744)

1809   Brazil exported the first shipment of coffee to Salem, Massachusetts.

1822   The French invented the first prototype Espresso machine.

1825   After the British took over Ceylon (Sri Lanka) from Dutch rule, aggressive coffee cultivation continued, clearing precious rain forests for coffee plantations.

1843   Paris had become a café society with 3,000 coffee houses established.

The history of coffee houses is the invention of clubs, was
that of the manners, the morals, and the politics of a people.
-ISAAC D'ISRAELI, CURIOSITIES OF LITERATURE, PUBLISHED IN LONDON IN 1824

In Sao Paulo, Brazil's coffee supply swelled. They produced half of the world's supply of coffee.

The manual coffee grinder was a staple item in US middle-class kitchens.

1855   *The Paris Exposition's biggest hit was a larger version of the prototype Espresso machine. Steam, the first great power source of the industrial age, fuelled the true child of the modern coffee era — the first steam-powered Espresso machine.*

1869   *A lethal fungus disease called coffee leaf rust spread and changed the balance of the world's coffee supply for the next 20 years.*

Approximately 176,000 acres of precious rain forest had been destroyed for the cultivation of coffee.

1873   *The first national coffee brand, a packaged roast ground coffee, was put on the US market by John Arbuckle.*

1876   *The original "iced coffee" appeared in Philadelphia.*

1879   *Due to the spread of the botanical disease, coffee leaf rust, coffee estates in India, Java, Sumatra and Malaysia were wiped out.*

By the late 18th century, Brazil, no longer under Portuguese colonial rule, supplied the world's coffee demand of 294,000 tons. For the first time since the Dutch had wrestled control over the coffee trade in the Middle East from the Arabs, another nation — Brazil — the king of coffee countries — ruled the "old" coffee world!

PART 3
ESPRESSO COFFEE RULES ... THE "NEW" WORLD

Coffee was confirmed as "the drink of democracy" by Café society during the European renaissance. Toward the turn of the 20th century, coffee houses were Europe's first public arenas, where people of both sexes and all classes could mingle independently, allowing for freedom of thought, public and political interchange. People shared thoughts and ideas and became aware of the exciting "new possibilities" available to them in the "new world".

Human awareness, driving desires and increasing inquisitiveness demanded heightened individual service – fast! With these coffee houses being the centers of learning, inspiration and places to exchange ideas, an embryo Espresso machine was born. A sudden unpredictable gust of change was about to transform coffee's destiny. Once again coffee's aromas brewed into a powerful storm called the "Espresso era" and the subsequent "cappuccino years".

Coffee beans continued to flourish as a cash crop around the world, and the explosion of Espresso coffee fueled this commodity force to another dramatic level of world demand. Omnipresent trading of coffee as a commodity can create national wealth or debt. Coffee has the power to fluctuate waves of foreign exchange for dozens of countries around the world. By the turn of the 21st century, Espresso coffee crowned a new era in coffee-drinking lifestyles and enterprise.

Espresso ... the fundamental element of today's popular fancy coffees ... is the continuum of coffee's karmic odyssey over the past millennium: alive, intense, stimulating and timeless.

THE EMERGENCE OF THE ESPRESSO ERA

1882 The New York Coffee Exchange commenced business.

1900 Coffee was often delivered door-to-door in the United States, by horse-pulled wagons! (A different version of today's coffee carts!)

1901 The first patent, by Bezzera, was filed for an Espresso coffee machine. Although the French first invented the prototype Espresso machine in 1843, using **steam** as the power source, it was the Italians who perfected it.

This patented machine contained a boiler and four "groups" of filters to hold dark fine coffee. The water boiled, and steam forced it through the groups of ground coffee, resulting in a brew which was stronger in flavor and body. Each cup of coffee was "expressly" made for one individual. This was "the birth of Espresso coffee".

1902   The first commercial Espresso machine was manufactured in Italy. Espresso soon became the quintessential coffee house beverage.

1903   Pavoni of Italy began to manufacture Espresso machines based on Bezzera's patent, and began to aggressively distribute them throughout Europe.

A German coffee importer discovered decaffeinated coffee, inventing a technique to strip the coffee of its caffeine, using clean water. He called his decaffeinated coffee "Sanka"; the French term "sans caffeine" translated means "without caffeine".

1910   "Dekafa", the first decaffeinated coffee imported from Germany, was first introduced to the United States market.

1911   United States Coffee Roasters was organized in St. Louis as an emergency-measure coffee supplier. This was the beginning of the National Coffee Association.

1915   War helped popularize coffee throughout the world. Red Cross wagons with coffee and doughnuts followed the troops in the two world wars. (These could have been the first coffee carts as well!)

1927   The first Espresso machine was installed in New York at Reggio's It is still on display there today.

1928   The Colombian Coffee Association was established.

1930   Reggio's Café in New York became a haven for artists and writers.

1933   Masterful Italian craftsmen fashioned copper and brass into tall, sculptured Espresso machines. These glistening, golden masterpieces, crowned with an elegant eagle, embodied the beginning of a new era, The Espresso Era.

| 1935 | Americans visiting Europe brought back eclectic Espresso souvenirs and an acquired appetite for continental coffee. This cross-culturing also fuelled more demand for the expansion of North American coffee houses. |

1938   Another Italian, Illy, created an Espresso machine that forced compressed air, rather than steam, through the dark, rich coffee grounds. This allowed for more control over the temperature level, which had an effect on the finished taste of the "expressly-made" Espresso coffee. A piston pump was also developed which forced hot, not boiling, water through the coffee. This eliminated the burnt taste of the earlier, more primitive, Espresso coffee.

1940   The National Coffee Association was christened, becoming a permanent national presence representing coffee roasters and importers throughout the US. The first coffee quota agreement was signed.

1946   The name "cappuccino" evolved from the resemblance of the drink to the chocolate brown color of the robes worn by the monks of the "Capuchin" order. The people of Rome creatively used the steam from the Espresso machines to heat milk, which was optionally added to their fragrant rich coffee. Since they were familiar with the Capuchin monks, the Italians decided to christen their beloved brew after the similar colored robes of the Capuchin monks.
Italians savored endless combinations of Espresso and steamed milk (cappuccino), consumed primarily in the morning, or in the evening with a sambuca or grappa (Italian brandy).

God created water, and man made cappuccino!
-SUSAN M. ZIMMER

Climbing prices in the 1940s led to a wave of new coffee plantings around the world, especially in Brazil, where new centers of coffee production emerged. The United States remained the world's dominant consumer of coffee.

1948   Gaggia of Italy began manufacturing a commercial spring piston-lever machine. This machine, with its long "lever" handle, allowed for nine times as much pressure as the steam method. It was capable of producing higher and more exact pressure upon the coffee grounds. This increased pressure blessed Espresso coffee with "crema" (or a layer of "foam") which floated on top of the Espresso coffee.

1950   Coffee bars begin to mushroom again in Britain, due to the success of the Espresso coffee machine. Italian immigrants brought their passion for Espresso coffee with them to America. This dark continental brew quickly began to change the national flavor preferences and its popularity expanded across the country.

Bars and coffee houses in San Francisco and New York's "Little Italy" catered to The Beat Generation. Writers, musicians and artists, wearing berets and sunglasses, passionately drank their strong, dark coffee while formulating and developing revolutions in art and literature.

In America, during the 1950s, coffee houses began to spawn as roadside diners and coffee shops.

The German daily ritual of afternoon coffee inspired the phrase "kaffeeklatsch", which means coffee talk or relaxed coffee gossip.

Viennese afternoon coffee moments attracted psychologists, inspired psychoanalysts, and brought modern physics to life.

Sometimes an Espresso, is just an Espresso!
-SIGMUND FREUD (1856-1939)

In Russia, France and England, coffee houses were the arenas where political revolutions were planned and nurtured.

1956   LaCimbali of Italy introduced the first "hydraulic" Espresso machine. It involved increased water pressure and advancements in precisely portioning the flow of water through the ground Espresso coffee.

The first-ever frappé was born in Greece, quite by chance. During a trade exhibition in Salonica, the second largest city in Greece, a drink for children was being promoted involving a mixture of milk, sugar and cold water in a shaker. Someone added a soluble instant coffee to the mix in the shaker and a cool, refreshing frappé with a special foam was born.

1959	Juan Valdez **became the** marketing face of Colombian Coffee.
1960	Faema of Italy **employed** an electric pump **to supply the pressure for the Espresso machine, rather than a manually operated piston.**
1961	The folk-era coffee houses of the sixties, **particularly in New York's Greenwich Village, birthed many budding poets, folk musicians and actors such as** James Taylor, Woody Allen, Arlo Guthrie and Pete Seeger. **(Similar to the first coffee houses in Turkey in AD 1554, and the Europeans in 1824!)**
	The music for coffee **did not end with Bach. The very first** Moog synthesizer **used in pop music was in a song called** "Percolator", **where the synthesizer imitated percolating coffee.**
1962	Coffee export quotas **were established on a worldwide basis, and the** International Coffee Agreement **was negotiated by the United Nations.**
1965	European cafes **and restaurants became creative with their coffee menus.** "Iced Coffees", **a refreshing parfait of** chilled continental coffee or Espresso, **ice cream and** whipped cream **topped with a** cherry and chocolate shavings, **are still popular today.**
1971	The first Starbucks coffee house **opened in Seattle's public market, creating a frenzy over freshly roasted whole-bean coffee.**
1972	Coffee prices began to fluctuate, **and the controls of the major coffee-producing countries disappeared.** Coffee became a speculative commodity, traded on the world markets **like petroleum and steel.**
1973	The first "fair trade" coffee **was imported to Europe** from Guatemala, Central America.
1975	The history of the coffee industry has been one of feast or famine, **for the small producers usually famine. Following a period of overproduction, relative to world demand, Brazil destroyed more than 10 billion pounds of coffee. This was done to prevent a glut in the market, and to keep coffee prices stable. Ironically, a** devastating coffee frost **followed. This sudden increase in world coffee demand propelled world coffee prices to the highest peak ever, with** costs rising over 500 percent.
1989	The International Coffee Agreement collapsed **when participating nations failed to sign a new pact. World coffee prices plunged to historic lows.**
1990	**Specialty coffee took off in the United States. Nestle launched a new retail product,** powdered instant "cappuccino", **in North America.**
1991	Starbucks went public **on the stock exchange. Gourmet coffee drinking, first popular in Seattle, gave rise to Espresso coffee bars across America. The national craving for specialty coffees and strong Espresso coffee evolved to become the** "Espresso explosion" of the nineties.

1994   Starbucks developed a relationship with Pepsi to create a cold coffee-based beverage. This kick-started "Iced or Frozen Cappuccino" in America (which had been popular in Europe since the 1960s).

1995   Organic coffee became the fastest growing segment of the specialty coffee market. Coffee and a "byte" booted into the 21st century, giving a whole new meaning to the word – coffee house! Cybercafes or internet cafes began to sprout around the world, as a place to grab a cup of joe, a sweet treat and park in front of a computer to surf the net, email, etc.

1996   Starbucks operated close to 2,000 retail locations nationwide and abroad, having exclusive relationships with airports, restaurants and hotels, with intentions for expansion to the same degree in Europe and Asia.

1997   Coffee pubs, serving a spectrum of specialty coffees, became more popular than the alcohol-serving bars and taverns. More than 50 percent of the Generation X'ers drank Espresso, cappuccinos and lattes. Close to 30 percent of this group drank iced or cold coffee beverages.

1998   108 million Americans (47 percent of the population) were drinking Espresso, cappuccino, latte, or iced/cold coffees as compared to 1997, when only 80 million (35 percent of the population) consumed these specialty coffee beverages – an increase of 28 million specialty coffee drinkers in one year!

2000   The veiled life of Saudi women in Saudi Arabia, still bound by tradition and Islamic law, was further restricted by regulations stating that police could arrest single women if they went into coffee houses without the written approval of a male guardian.

2001   Earthquake disaster brought commerce to a halt in San Salvador – wiping out precious coffee fields – the most relied upon industry for income.

2002   Since the first cybercafe opened in 1984, thousands of these "net-cafes" (not Nescafe!) now offer people around the world "Coffee with a Byte"! From the "Surf 'n' Sip" to the "Mudhouse e-café", these trendy popular meeting places combine the comfort of a coffee house, restaurant or bar with the many applications of the internet.

Coffee and its Espresso descendants possess a passionate spirit and timeless karma, which have always been, and always will be.

The market price of a food product simply cannot provide the information needed to protect the land and the people who farm it. It ignores vital information – the costs to the land, soil, and human health – on which our ultimate survival depends.

-FRANCES MOORE LAPPE, FOOD, FARMING AND DEMOCRACY (1990)

COFFEE'S FUTURE

THE SCOOP ON SUSTAINABLE COFFEE

The term "sustainable" has been around for a long time now. Only recently has a new surge of interest about sustainable coffees been introduced into the mainstream of gourmet coffee drinkers. A decade ago, international groups such as the United Nations broadly defined a sustainable product as: "those products which are produced and fulfill current needs, in such a way, that it does not damage the capacity of future generations to satisfy theirs".

Sustainable coffee production is a very complex canopy of environmentally sensitive issues, from the coffee farm to the consumer's cup. Sustainable coffee is coffee grown and harvested in a way that adheres to the following criteria:

– Non-use of herbicides and pesticides

– Effective use of shade tree coverage and conservation of natural resources

– Fair treatment of workers

These concerns are structured into an exclusive specialty coffee niche, focus-specific on the strictest quality standards. Conscientious consumers are demanding products grown and processed within environmentally sound and socially just parameters.

The sustainable coffee categories are: certified organic, certified shade-grown and certified fair trade coffees which are policed by third-party independent agencies. These agencies, for example, the Quality Assurance International (QAI) for certified organic coffee, Transfair Fair TradeMark Canada; Transfair USA for certified fair trade coffee, and the Smithsonian Migratory Bird Center (SMBC), have developed strict criteria for the participating conscientious coffee producers, traders and roasting companies to follow.

Inspectors from these organizations independently inspect the operations of growers and roasters to determine whether or not they are adhering to certain strict standards. If they are, they receive the right to market their coffee under a certification label. All this comes with a price tag, since these conscientious coffee companies must pay the price for yearly membership, inspection fees and privilege user fees. It also takes more time and labor to grow organic or shade-grown coffees. Despite all of this, more than 40 percent of companies have become certified. Once again, enterprising individuals and groups can smell the aroma of opportunity in supplying consumer demands.

The coffee industry as a whole is taking extraordinary measures to create expanded awareness and open communication channels for this specialized coffee niche. From coffee growers to importers, from roasters to retailers, they are collectively joining forces to embrace "sustainability" as a key business theme, in order to provide better-quality coffee for consumers, the environment and for socio-economic reasons. International conferences are also being planned around these issues. For example, The Specialty Coffee Association of America (SCAA) recently signed an agreement with the United States Agency for Development (USAID) to ensure future development projects in coffee-growing regions focus on producing higher-quality specialty coffees. This sustainable coffee phenomenon is resonating with concerned gourmet coffee consumers. As coffee producers learn more about the social impact of changing tastes, concerns, responsibilities and demands, we can expect new, healthier harvests and better-quality sustainable specialty coffees to satisfy our national passion.

> Consumers have more control over the food chain than many of us think. Since the free-market system respects buying power above all else, consumers need to speak the language the market recognizes. That means expressing a clear choice about how we want our food grown, processed and delivered to us and whom we want to profit from the conduct of trade.
>
> –MYRNA GREENFIELD, MAKING COFFEE STRONG (1994)

CERTIFIED ORGANIC COFFEE

No doubt about it, we know what the future holds . . . it's going to be organic! New practices have begun to be initiated around the world for food growers, be it for fruits, vegetables, herbs or coffee. This is not some virtual off-the-planet New Age concept, it's reality — organic farming. Organically grown coffee is a healthy "good-for-you" product grown without chemicals, artificial pesticides, herbicides or fertilizers. The absence of chemicals also enhances the soil's productivity and regeneration.

- Certified organic coffee must come from independently certified farms, be purchased by certified importers, and roasted by certified roasters, to maintain the integrity of the organically grown coffee beans.
- These organic coffee beans are tracked as they move from the organic source to the organic coffee cup.
- Organic coffee farmers focus on maintaining good soil quality and plant health as the most effective means to boost productivity and maintain immunity against disease.
- Currently there are only four certified organic farm roasters in the United States. They adhere to strict organic rules, from using clean biomass fuels, like sawdust pellets, which do not contribute to global warming, to rules of recycling the heat used in roasting the beans.
- Organic coffee companies only purchase and sell coffee which has been grown without synthetic agrochemicals.
- Many US states are regulating organic coffee to ensure its quality, and the United States Development Agency plans to enforce additional regulation under the US Organic Food Production Act.
- The most powerful enforcer of organic claims, however, is third-party certification such as Quality Assurance International. Other respected organizations include: the Organic Crop Improvement Association (OCAIA), Farm Verified Organic, Eco-OK and the Demeter Association, which certify organic and shade-grown coffees.
- Certified organic coffee is currently the leader in the sustainable coffee category with estimated sales between $75-$125 million dollars, based on the Specialty Coffee Association and other organic industry sources.
- Certified organic coffees are priced at a premium since they take more time and labor to grow, not to mention all of the memberships and fees.
- Mexico is the world's leading supplier of certified organic coffee, and its overall the fourth largest coffee producer. The majority of all the small coffee farms in Mexico are owned by indigenous people.

SHADE-GROWN COFFEE

Shade-grown coffee is a method of growing in an agroforest (almost forest-like conditions) whereby coffee shrubs are grown and cultivated under a natural canopy of other trees and crop species, such as fruit (banana) trees, along with a host of various non-coffee products. These coffee agroforestry systems create a natural habitat sanctuary for migratory birds to land, eat, rest and continue on their journeys. These agroforests also offer the advantage of protection for the tropical forests in the countries where coffee is produced.

- A single shade coffee agroforest can support 66 species of trees and shrubs and 73 wildlife species.
- Certain types of coffee help preserve the flora and fauna, and a full polyculture of trees, sometimes called "coffee gardens".
- Certified shade-grown coffee sales are estimated between $3-$6 million according to reports from industry roasters and the Smithsonian Migratory Bird Center.
- The Smithsonian Migratory Bird Center (SMBC) established a shade coffee criteria system for organic coffee farmers. The SMBC became involved in the coffee industry after the discovery of a decline in migratory bird populations, attributed to the changeover in coffee-farming practices from shade tree to sun farming.
- The issues that coffee plantations should serve as a source for biodiversity was brought forth by the First Sustainable Coffee Congress in 1996, sponsored by the Smithsonian Migratory Bird Center. (Biodiversity is linked with the rational use of agrochemicals in coffee production, and concerns for the existence of other trees within and around the agroforest.)

Coffee is consumed furiously in the richest of countries,
yet in contrast is grown with few exceptions
in the poorest parts of the globe!
-G. DICUM/N. LUTTINGER, THE COFFEE BOOK (1999)

FAIR TRADE COFFEE

Fair Trade certified coffee is part of the global Fair Trade movement which focuses primarily on paying producers fair wages for the products they produce. Integrity and equality is also sought in building a strong rapport between producers, traders and consumers.

Fair Trade coffee was conceived in the 1970s and founded by people who were frustrated and uneasy with the social and economic impact of the coffee trade. Since the movement spread, in the late 1990s, into mainstream consumer discourse in Europe, the inherited concerns have steadily been growing in North America. Particular concerns focus on inconsistent, low wages for coffee-picking workers who must carry heavy sacks of coffee cherries through long hot days. Coffee farmers receive only 10 percent of the retail price of their coffee, and may earn only $5 per day or less for tending their coffee crop.

The Fair Trade Federation identified these concerns and established some principles:
– fair wages to the producers and pickers
– cooperative workplaces
– consumer education
– environmental sustainability
– financial/technical support during poor growing cycles.

- Fair wages paid to the coffee producers means that coffee workers are paid a living wage which will cover their basic needs, including food, shelter, education and health care for their families.
- In many countries, producers are paid a fair price for their coffee products directly from Fair Trade organizations and Fair Trade coffee companies in consuming nations. This enables them to bypass the middlemen banditos, called "coyotes" in Central America. These coyotes are guilty of unethical power plays on helpless coffee farmers who are indebted to them for financial assistance. In many remote villages the poor peasant producers have only the coyotes to turn to for financial assistance between harvest when food supplies are exhausted.
- Currently, more than 500,000 farmers in 17 countries produce and sell more than 32 million pounds of coffee each year through the Fair Trade network.
- Social conditions are a prime consideration for the Fair Trade coffee producers. The guaranteed payment of a minimum base price for coffee is above US $1.41 per pound for organic coffee, regardless of the world market price. The rules and membership of Fair Trade are managed by the non-profit certification organization called Transfair USA which is certified by their Fair Trade seal. Max Havelaar has also developed Fair Trade Certification marks for Fair Trade coffees.
- Fair wages do not necessarily mean that the consumer pays more for Fair Trade coffee. Since the participating organizations work directly with the producers, they are able to cut costs and return a greater percentage of the retail price to the producers.

Coffee — a new compassionate purpose
is "grounds" for hope for Coffee Kids.
-Susan M. Zimmer

COFFEE KIDS

Coffee Kids is an international non-profit organization established to improve the quality of life for children and families who live in impoverished coffee-growing communities around the world. Coffee Kids works hand-in-hand with local partner organizations around the world to develop long-term programs that address community needs ranging from health care to economic development.

Coffee comes from growing coffee communities, where literally millions of people dedicate their lives to growing coffee for the rest of the coffee-consuming world. Tragically, the blessings of coffee do not always filter down to the people who grow it. These coffee-producing farmers earn as little as a penny a pound for their coffee. Even during successful harvests, the children of coffee growers go without many basic needs that are often taken for granted, such as education, adequate food and water, and clothing.

Coffee Kids was founded by Bill Fishbein, who travelled to Guatemala twelve years ago and came face to face with the realities of coffee and poverty. After returning to the United States from his travels, he founded this organization as a means of linking passionate coffee drinkers and coffee-related businesses, to give something back to the impoverished families who grow coffee for us to enjoy.

A20 CALGARY HERALD Saturday, October 14, 2000 **CANADA**

Coffee-brewing cars drive of the future

KATE JAIMET
OTTAWA CITIZEN
OTTAWA

* By the end of the decade, drivers will be using the exhaust from their car engines to brew cappuccino on the dashboard, physicist and futurist Amory Lovins predicts.

The cars of the future will be powered by fuel cells that combine hydrogen and oxygen to produce electricity, then spew out hot water as their only waste product, Lovins said Friday.

"Your car will emit nothing but hot drinking water, will work better, save money and use no oil," he said. "Hydrogen cars will save more oil worldwide than Saudi Arabia now sells."

Lovins will be giving the keynote address Sunday at the United Nations Environment Program's seminar on cleaner production in Montreal. Among the things he has designed are a greenhouse plantation to grow bananas in the Rocky Mountains and an ultra-light, ultra-efficient "hypercar" that runs on hydrogen.

Amory Lovins

"The old car industry will be toast in 20 years," predicted the environmentalist and adviser to the automobile industry.

The cars Lovins dreams of will use one-third the energy of today's cars, and will be made of ultra-light, carbon-fibre material that is aerodynamically designed to minimize air resistance.

In this futuristic scenario, drivers will fill up their tanks with hydrogen gas. An on-board fuel cell will combine the hydrogen with oxygen molecules from the air, creating a chemical reaction that will generate electricity to power the car.

But the reaction won't deplete the Earth's oxygen supply, Lovins said, because the oxygen will come out the exhaust pipe as water.

"You're not depleting anything. It's a closed loop."

General Motors already has a prototype hydrogen-powered car, but the company is still years away from putting such a car on the market, said spokeswoman Faye Roberts.

"Assuming everything works, we'd start high-volume production in 2004, but we wouldn't expect to see high-volume sales until 2009."

Honda is also working on their FCX-V3 hydrogen-powered vehicle, said public relations co-ordinator Anton Yewshyn-Pawczuk. It's one of many high-tech alternatives the auto industry is exploring, including hybrid gasoline-electric cars that are just starting to come on the market.

Ford demonstrated its prototype P-2000 hydrogen-powered car on Parliament Hill this past May, and hopes to have one on the market by 2004.

The hydrogen to fuel these cars would be derived from splitting atoms of water, using electricity. But one of the major hurdles is how to distribute hydrogen fuel to consumers.

Lovins believes that hurdle will be overcome as more businesses and homes move to hydrogen fuel as a source of electricity. As the demand for hydrogen rises, market forces will ensure the supply.

Nothing in itself is poison or cure,
everything depends on the dosage.

-PARACELSUS, A RENAISSANCE PHYSICIAN (1493-1541)

CAFFEINE AND THE COFFEE BEAN

CAFFEINE POWER

Sipping, savoring and being stimulated by society's most beloved traditional tonic has become a lifestyle for many of us. This caffeine-charged cup of "I'm-worth-it" does more than just give your day a lift! It is capable of changing many of our physiological responses. With coffee being the world's second most popular beverage, next to water, the health concerns over caffeine-rich coffee are minimal in proportion to the amounts of coffee consumed worldwide.

The straight talk on the java-jive is that it can be enjoyed with no cause for concern if consumption is kept in moderation.

Average coffee drinkers who consume at least two cups of coffee, Espresso, cappuccino or a regular cup of joe, enjoy mild physiological short-term effects. Caffeine has the ability to: stimulate the brain, reduce irritability, may improve mood, postpone fatigue; make one feel brighter and enhance alertness. It also increases metabolism and concentration span, stimulates respiration, increases gastric secretion and urination. (Evidently, the effects depend on the personalities of the coffee drinkers, their environment, and even the time of day.)

On the other side of the cup, habitual coffeeholics, consuming larger doses of up to 700 mg of caffeine a day – equivalent to eight or nine average cups, may experience long-term effects. Certainly at this level, and beyond, coffee drinkers may suffer from chronic insomnia, persistent anxiety, lightheadedness and, sometimes, depression. (Personally, I would be afraid that this amount of coffee per day would peel the enamel off my teeth!)

Even larger doses of caffeine, for example 10 cups of "strong" coffee, consumed all at once, can be toxic, causing abnormally rapid heartbeat, fever, chills, convulsions and even delirium. The lethal dose of caffeine is approximately 10 grams, equivalent to 100 cups of coffee.

No study has ever found a life-threatening disease to be linked to consuming the caffeine in coffee. Important and interesting aspects of coffee drinking and your health will be explained in the following chapter.

As Paracelsus said . . . "everything depends on the dosage". The key understanding here is "sip and savor in moderation".

Voltaire, the great philosopher, was warned that coffee was a "slow poison". The 80-year old philosopher replied "I think it must be slow. I've been drinking it for 65 years and I'm not dead yet!"

-VOLTAIRE, FRENCH PHILOSOPHER (1694-1778)

CAFFEIN-ATION INFORMATION

CAFFEINE POWER

- Caffeine is the world's most popular drug.
- Caffeine is an odorless, bitter compound of the purine alkaloid family.
- Caffeine is found in over 60 plants: kola nuts, used in the preparation of cola drinks; cocoa bean pods, hence in cocoa and chocolate products; hundreds of tea leaf species.
- The caffeine content of coffee beans varies according to the species of the coffee plant. Coffee beans from the arabica plant, grown mostly in Central and South America, contain about 1.1 percent caffeine. Beans from the robusta plant, grown mostly in Indonesia and Africa, contain approximately 2.2 percent caffeine.
- The body absorbs caffeine. It appears in body tissues about 5 minutes after it is ingested. It reaches its highest levels 30 to 60 minutes after ingestion. It takes the body 3 to 6 hours to eliminate half the caffeine ingested (caffeine's half-life).
- The body can absorb and process 150 to 200 mg of caffeine (approximately 2 cups of coffee) per hour.
- In general, *Espresso coffee contains less caffeine* than filtered coffees because there is just a small amount of water passing through a small amount of coffee grounds in a shorter period of time. Evidently, less caffeine ends up in the beverage! *Unfortunately, many people confuse intense flavor with high caffeine content.* Finer grinds of coffee can increase the dose of the caffeine which is extracted form the coffee, because there is a larger surface area of coffee, per unit volume, for the water to pass through.
- The amount of caffeine extracted from an Espresso is around 80 to 85 percent.
- There is less caffeine in a small Espresso than in any other coffee beverage. There is less caffeine in a regular coffee made with arabica than the same size cup of coffee made with robusta beans. Therefore, *drink less of the best!*
- A darker roasted coffee bean contains less caffeine than a lighter roast since the higher temperatures required for the darker roast eliminate more of the caffeine in the bean!
- Almost 80 percent of American adults drink 2 cups (500 mL) of coffee (200 mg caffeine) a day.
- Annual consumption of caffeine is about 120,000 tonnes — equivalent to 70 mg of the drug a day for each consumer. Of this total, 54 percent is in the form of, or derived from, coffee, 43 percent from tea.
- Canadian consumption is close to 2,200 tonnes a year (244 mg/2½ cups a day) for each person. Of this total, 55 percent of this caffeine is consumed in the form of coffee, and about 32 percent in the form of tea. (Soft drinks, cocoa and chocolate products, and medicinal uses account for the remainder).
- Caffeine does have a pharmacological action. This was discovered in the early 19th century. It is still being used today as an analgesic. Of course, this is at doses very much higher than the amounts contained in a normal cup of coffee.

COMPARATIVE CAFFEINE CHART

SUBSTANCE	CAFFEINE (MILLIGRAMS)
1 large shot of Espresso (2 oz./60 mL)	45-100 mg
1 cup brewed (filtered) coffee (6 oz./170 mL)	60-120 mg
1 cup instant coffee (6 oz./170 mL)	70 mg
1 cup decaffeinated coffee (6 oz./170 mL)	1-5 mg
1 cup tea, 3-minute steep (6 oz./170 mL)	40 mg
1 can caffeinated soda (12 oz./340 mL)	38-45 mg
1 glass chocolate milk (6 oz./170 mL)	4 mg
1 square dark chocolate (1 oz./30 g)	20 mg
1 square milk chocolate (1 oz./30 g)	6 mg
1 tablet caffeinated cold remedy	25-50 mg
Anacin - 2 doses	64 mg
1 diet tablet	75-200 mg
1 can 7-Up (12 oz./340 mL)	0 mg

Drinking decaf doesn't mean selling out on flavor, aroma or quality . . . it should taste the same as caffeinated coffee if the caffeine is removed properly . . .

-Rosemary Furfaro, *Drinking Decaffeinated Coffees*

FOR THE LOVE OF DECAF
(De-Caffeination Information)

"Madam, would you like coffee, mint tea or 'the un-coffee'?" Many people these days are choosing to drink the "un-coffee"! Decaffeinated coffee appeals to a certain kind of coffee-lover, those with sensitive stomachs, those who find regular coffee too stimulating or those whose sleep will be ruined by a "leaded" coffee nightcap. To most dyed-in-the-wool caffeine drinkers, drinking the "unleaded brew" just doesn't have that same psychological "kick" as the "regular leaded brew". The fact remains that, even though the caffeine molecule, in its naked state, is a bitter alkaloid, caffeine loses its potency during the decaffeination and roasting processes. Flavor and aroma compounds can also be diminished or removed in the decaffeination process. Although decaffeinated coffee beans are difficult to roast, it is usually the roasting process itself, if not done properly, that is responsible for the unpleasant tastes and textures of some decaf coffees! A superior decaffeination process, however, protects the original, rich flavor characteristics of the coffee when the caffeine is removed.

Based on my personal experience, a superior, 100 percent arabica, quality "air-roasted", Swiss-water decaffeinated coffee, can deliver a deliciously satisfying cup of decaf Espresso or filtered coffee. I believe it could challenge any comparative taste test with a standard cup of caffeinated coffee.

The decaffeinated coffee market is achieving exponential growth. Today, it accounts for more than 20 percent of America's coffee consumption, as compared to only 3 percent back in 1962! Hence, greater demands for quality and variety go along with increased health concerns.

In an effort to make the best choices to suit personal preferences, we need to understand the various technological processes used by the coffee industry. The following general overview and information may help.

A superior decaffeination process does for decaf coffee . . .
what virtual did for reality.
-SWISS WATER DECAFFEINATED COFFEE COMPANY INC.

DECAFFEINATION PROCESSING METHODS

The process of decaffeinating coffee began at the turn of the 20th century. Although there have been many patents since then, today there are only three primary decaffeination methods used by the coffee industry. Each process begins the same way: the green (unroasted) coffee beans are moistened with steam and water to soften them, opening their pores (becoming porous), and loosening the caffeine bonds. After this initial step, the following various methods are used. These methods are conventionally named according to the process:

1 – The "Swiss Water Process" or "Water only" method
2 – The solvent (chemical or natural) method
3 – The supercritical carbon dioxide (pressurized gas) method

THE SWISS WATER PROCESS "WATER ONLY" METHOD

Swiss Water decaffeination processing almost always uses high-quality arabica beans. Thus, the final higher-quality product is reflected in a more expensive price tag. You get what you pay for!

This process does not use chemicals. First, the caffeine, as well as the flavor extracts, is stripped from the beans by the initial water and steam soak. This first batch of beans is discarded. The water, which now holds the coffee flavor extracts and caffeine, is filtered through carbon filters to remove the caffeine. Now only the "coffee-flavor-charged" extract (caffeine free) solution remains. It is this "coffee-flavor-charged" extract which is used to subsequently absorb the caffeine from a new batch of beans. Due to the scientific principles of solubility, the caffeine moves from an area of higher concentration (the bean itself), to an area of lower concentration (the extract). In this process, 94 to 96 percent of the caffeine is removed. Since this process uses no chemicals, it is referred to as an organic or natural method.

In a non-Swiss Water decaffeination process, sometimes chemicals, rather than charcoal filters, are used to extract the caffeine from the "coffee-flavor-charged" extract. It is important to note that the chemical solvent does not come into contact with the coffee beans. The coffee comes into contact with water only, and the rich aroma and flavor characteristics of the coffee are minimally altered.

THE SOLVENT METHOD

• Certain selective solvents, such as methylene chloride and common ethyl acetate, are the most widely used chemical compounds to decaffeinate coffee.
• Although synthetic methylene chloride has been under fire with regards to being hazardous to the environment, its use is allowed providing the residues fall below certain limits.
• Ethyl acetate may be sourced from natural ingredients and it can be produced synthetically as well. This method is generally advertised as "naturally" decaffeinated process. Unfortunately, there is no way of knowing whether the solvent source is natural or synthetic.

Solvent Touches the Bean Method: *After the initial moistened phase, the solvent circulates through the beans, removing the caffeine. The beans are then rinsed with water, steamed once more, thereby easily evaporating any residual solvent, and dried. The beans are then sold to be roasted, and the extracted caffeine is sold for medicinal uses and soft drinks. This chemical caffeine method removes 96 to 98 percent of the caffeine.*

Solvent "Never" Touches the Bean Method: *After the initial moistened phase, when the hot water bath has soaked the caffeine and the coffee extracts from the beans, the "flavor-charged" water is separated from the stripped beans. The flavor-charged water is now combined with a solvent, which unites with the caffeine. The solvent carrying the caffeine is now separated out, and the flavor-charged caffeine-free water is reunited with the stripped coffee beans, to reabsorb the coffee flavors and oils.*

It is important to note that the solvent here never touches the bean itself. Again, any residual solvent is evaporated in the final steaming phase, or during the roasting process of the coffee bean.

THE "SUPERCRITICAL" CARBON DIOXIDE (Pressurized Gas) METHOD

Once again, after the initial moistening phase, the coffee beans which are being decaffeinated are put into an extractor. Pressurized "supercritical" carbon dioxide is used at 250 to 300 times its normal atmospheric pressure. Carbon dioxide at this pressure turns somewhat into a fluid, having a form between a liquid and a gas. When this "supercritical" fluid/gas solvent passes through the coffee beans, the caffeine migrates to the solvent.

When the caffeine removal is complete, the now caffeine-rich solvent passes through a filter, to absorb the caffeine for reuse. When its work is done, and the pressure released, the fluid/gas solvent turns into gas and dissipates. Carbon dioxide is inexpensive to obtain and is non-toxic. This supercritical carbon dioxide method removes 96 to 98 percent of the caffeine without removing other coffee flavor characteristics.

Interestingly enough, there are only a small number of these decaffeination processing plants in the world since they are very, very expensive to operate. (This is also one reason why decaffeinated coffee is more expensive to purchase than regular coffee.)

CONSUMER AWARENESS: ADS AND LABELING OF DECAF COFFEE

The Food and Drug Administration requires that coffee must have 97 percent of the caffeine removed from the untreated green beans in order to be labeled "decaffeinated".

When you are purchasing decaffeinated coffee, check to see if the decaf coffee is arabica or robusta blend. Depending on the type of decaf coffee bean, and/or coffee bean blend, the amount of caffeine left in the finished product can also vary. For example, the amount of caffeine in a decaffeinated 100 percent robusta coffee will be naturally higher than a 100 percent arabica coffee, since robusta beans have almost twice as much caffeine in their natural state as arabica coffee beans.

It is interesting to note, however, that the majority of caffeine-free coffee sold in specialty stores is initially shipped to decaffeinating plants in Switzerland and Germany. It is in these countries that the majority of all decaffeinated coffees are produced. Once the processing is complete, they are then shipped back to North America. Decaffeinated coffee originated in Germany over 100 years ago. It may be comforting to know that the processing standards are scrupulous and the quality controls of their decaffeination facilities are superior.

Traditionally, inferior robusta beans are chosen for decaffeination because they yield a higher caffeine by-product which is sold for medicinal and soft drink purposes. However, more and more superior arabica coffee beans are being decaffeinated, for their superior finished coffee flavor, aroma and body, and certainly for the greatest benefit, a lower-caffeine coffee product!

NOW – DECAF COFFEE OR MINT TEA ANYONE?

Before we switch forever from decaf coffee to mint tea, concerned and careful consumers may be consoled to know the following facts:

- Methylene chloride evaporates at 180°F (83°C)
- Beans are roasted to at least 350°F (180°C)
- Coffee is brewed between 190 and 212°F (88 and 100°C)
  Therefore, the amount of methylene chloride left in brewed decaf coffee is, in parts per billion, less than is in the air of many North American cities. Personally, I would be more concerned about fumes from a passing motorized vehicle before I would have any anguish over my cup of decaf!

"Looks like we're the victims of corporate sabotage. Someone has been making decaf!"

Electric Espresso, page 92

Cupid Cappuccino, page 132

. . . the drink called "COFFEE", having many excellent virtues, closes the orifice of the Stomach, fortifies the heat within, helpeth Digestion, quickeneth the Spirits, maketh the heart lightsome, is good against Eyesores, Coughs or Colds, Rhumes, Consumptions, Headache, Dropsy, Gout, Scurvy, King's Evil, and many others . . .

-THE PUBLICK ADVISER (1657), ENGLISH NEWSPAPER ADVERTISEMENT (COFFEE DESCRIBED AS CURE ALL)

COFFEE AND YOUR HEALTH

COFFEE – A CUP OF HEALTH?

Since its genesis, coffee has been regarded in centuries-old medicinal theories, as an "elixir of life" as well as a "poison". Controversies on the effects of coffee on human health continue today, and a vague aura of confusion still surrounds these opinions, good and bad.

No other drink has been so carefully researched for possible effects on the human body, nor has any other drink received so much media attention in this respect. Coffee and caffeine, its chief component, have been measured, analyzed and tested in every possible way. Coffee has certain positive values in stimulating the mind, however, coffee's role as an actual medicinal aid has certainly been exaggerated.

During the 1980s major news stories linked coffee drinking with diseases of every kind: cancers, heart diseases, infertility, etc. Subsequent studies and scientific research have provided very little evidence linking coffee to such serious harmful effects. Recently, "The Wellness Letter", produced by the University of California, stated that coffee has received a bad rap, and that it can be enjoyed in moderation.

The general consensus is that in moderation (four or five cups a day) coffee is not harmful to the proper functioning of the human body. Most importantly, though, is the fact that each individual differs as to his or her own caffeine sensitivity. Some people are immune to five or more cups a day of their favorite brew, and can drink it late into the evening without losing sleep. Other individuals may not be able to tolerate coffee and caffeine whatsoever. Some could actually be allergic to coffee. Physical and physiological reactions to the caffeine in coffee can vary tremendously from individual to individual.

There is no question that coffee is a stimulant. It provides temporary energy by stimulating the nervous system and metabolism. On the other hand, caffeine also occurs naturally in the leaves, seeds or fruits of over 60 plants. Caffeine has been part of our lives for thousands of years.

It may be helpful to know and explore some of the following important aspects of coffee drinking and your health.

The powers of a man's mind are directly proportional
to the quantities of coffee he drank!
-Sir James MacKintosh, Scottish philosopher (1765-1832)

MENTAL PERFORMANCE

Coffee, in general, does give one a "perk-me-up"! Three to five cups a day stimulates the nervous system, increases memory and quickens reaction time. This was proven in tests conducted by the British National Health Institute. Further research data has found that caffeine stimulates the brain's alertness and the ability to maintain attention, even on long and tedious jobs. It also has positive effects on one's general mood.

Current research has proven that caffeine naturally contains anti-headache components which help diminish headaches by increasing the blood flow feeding the heart, while constricting blood vessels in the head. (Thus it is not surprising to note that caffeine is the most common medicinal ingredient used in headache preparations and other pain relievers.)

Drinking coffee at night may help certain workers increase safety, enhance hand-eye coordination and reduce accidents, for instance air traffic controllers and pilots; jobs where intense powers of concentration and sharp reflexes are required.

CAFFEINE AND EXERCISE PERFORMANCE

Caffeine has caused much debate in the sporting world. In fact, the International Olympic Committee considers caffeine a "performance enhancer". Some studies attribute to caffeine the stimulation of energy production, but this effect may be the result of an increase in psychological motivation.

A study published in 1993, in the American Sports Medicine magazine analyzed the use of caffeine in sports and made two interesting conclusions. The first is that there is no certain data to prove that caffeine determines an increase of muscle strength in brief, strenuous exercises. Secondly, caffeine is "invigorating" for prolonged, moderately strenuous exercises of over half an hour. Thus, it may improve performance in sports where rapid movements and reactions are required, such as boxing. However, it can be detrimental in cases where a firm hold is needed, like archery or fencing.

A general boost to overall endurance has made coffee drinking popular among cyclists and marathon runners, however, the downside is its diuretic effect, increasing the frequency of urination, thus dehydrating the body, which can have a negative effect on athletes.

THE "CHOLESTEROL" ISSUE

An alarm bell was rung years ago in the Scandinavian countries, concerning an increase in blood cholesterol in habitual coffee drinkers. The result of the Norwegian Tromsoe Heart Study, conducted on 14,500 people, found that coffee increased their blood cholesterol. They had also proven, however, in 1994, that the results were dependent on the coffee's preparation method, and that the cholesterol increase only occurred when BOILED COFFEE was consumed, NOT filtered coffee, Espresso or coffee prepared with an Espresso coffee pot.

Boiled or percolated coffee produces a lipid component of coffee which was linked to a rise in cholesterol levels in the above noted report. This link had no connection to the specific caffeine in the coffee, rather to the by-products resulting from the brewing method used in the experiment. Further studies and experiments have proven that using paper filters reduces this problem, since the by-products are trapped on the filters as the coffee passes through them.

TO THE BEAT OF YOUR HEART

The keyword is moderation. Four or five cups a day do not interfere with the heart's proper functioning, despite the fact that it has long been commonly thought that coffee, being a mild stimulant, would lead to various forms of heart disease.

Studies which have focused on the risk of coronary disease, irregular heartbeats and heart attacks, have found no significant association between such diseases and drinking coffee. Study after study, of which the following are only a few, have found no connecting links.

- A 25-year study, between 1966 and 1991, involving 103,000 people in six countries, published by Martin Myers and Antono Basinki in Toronto, strongly concluded that coffee consumption does not contribute to heart disease.
- A 1990 Harvard Heart Professionals' Study, of 45,000 men found no link between coffee, caffeine and cardiovascular heart disease or stroke, in men who drank four or more cups of coffee per day.
- In publication data from the Nurses' Health Study, which had tracked the dietary habits of more than 85,000 female nurses since 1980, the results clearly stated that caffeine did not increase heart disease.
- In 1974, a 12-year study, the Framingham Heart Study, concluded that there was no association between coffee and heart attacks.
- According to Rotterdam University, which has conducted studies on the correlation between coronary heart disease, heart attacks and drinking coffee, no significant association between such diseases and drinking coffee has been found.

It is common practice, and most certainly if it is advised by your medical professional, to decrease or eliminate coffee from the diet if signs of cardiac arrhythmia and/or palpitations occur. Listen to your heart's counsel and drink coffee only in moderation.

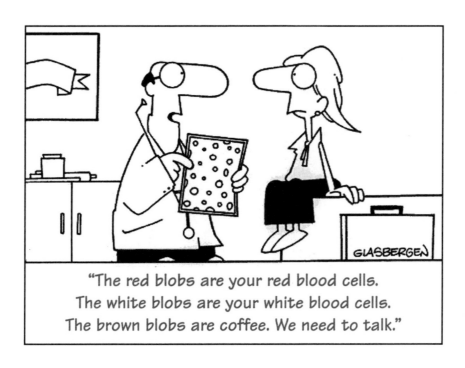

"The red blobs are your red blood cells.
The white blobs are your white blood cells.
The brown blobs are coffee. We need to talk."

COFFEE AND ULCERS

Recent studies have shown that most ulcers are caused by Helicobacter pylori, a bacteria. Coffee, along with spicy foods, may aggravate an existing ulcer, however, IT IS NOT THE CAUSE! I believe that stress is most times the core culprit behind the brewing of an ulcer. Perhaps drinking coffee excessively to the point of having "coffee nerves", when an ulcer is present, may delay the healing and aggravate it more. I, have had many an ulcer, however, they never gave me a reason to stop drinking my beloved brew!

In fact, Vitamin B3 (niacin) affects the metabolism of the gastric and intestinal area and, ironically, our daily needs may be supplied by one cup of coffee. Niacin is a valuable component in coffee, and one cup contains the recommended daily requirement.

SLEEPLESS NIGHTS

Personally, I have had many of these in my life, and I do agree with one of the most stereotypical claims that "coffee keeps you awake". Over and over again scientific research replies, "It depends on the individual". It has never been documented that coffee regularly causes insomnia, unless it is drunk in large quantities at night, because of the half-life of caffeine (that is the time it takes for the body to eliminate half of the substance), which is 3 to 4 hours. In general, however, the effects of caffeine on sleep patterns have been studied, and it usually shortens overall sleep time, delays sleep onset, and reduces the depth of sleep. One can be more easily aroused during sleep, and the quality of sleep is also diminished. In Scandinavia, however, coffee is drunk right at bedtime and is considered to be conducive to promoting good sleep! Once again, these effects can vary, and relate to each individual's tolerance of caffeine.

They say the elderly are more sensitive to the effects of coffee than are young people. Then again, I am perplexed as to why Ruth, my mother-in-law, who is in her 70's (keeping in mind 75 is middle-aged!), can drink one or two cups of regular coffee with her after-dinner dessert, and still is able to sleep at night1

. . . STILL IT IS BEYOND DOUBT THAT COFFEE CAUSES CONSIDERABLE EXCITEMENT IN THE BRAIN!

-(Jean) Anthelme Brillat-Savarin (1755-1826), French jurist and gourmet, Gastronomical meditation

COFFEE, MOM AND BABY

With regard to drinking coffee during pregnancy, most medical professionals recommend that pregnant women avoid any drugs, including caffeine.

"Pregnancy and coffee-drinking" has received a good deal of attention from researchers, since 80 percent of American women drink coffee while expecting a baby.

As published in the Journal of the American Medical Association, studies have reassured expectant mothers that in consuming 300 milligrams of caffeine per day (the equivalent of three to four cups/750 mL to 1 L of coffee), they stood no greater risk of premature births, low-birthweight babies, or malformations at birth than women who abstained.

Moderate coffee drinking creates no risk for fertility. There is more serious concern and a direct association between heavy coffee drinking by female smokers. In other words, it is most likely to be the smoking habit, not coffee, which impairs a woman's chance of having children.

DIETING WITH COFFEE

A cup of black coffee contains only two calories, with a dash of milk it contains approximately 10 calories. If you add one teaspoon of sugar to the coffee and milk, you have approximately 20 calories in that cup of coffee.

A cup of coffee on an empty stomach alleviates the hunger sensation. Coffee is by no means a slimming substance, but it has been proven that caffeine stimulates the body's production of energy. The body is a machine that burns fuel to obtain the energy needed to produce work and heat. Caffeine speeds up the body's general metabolism and causes calories to burn up faster.

According to a recent study, 450 milligrams (approximately four to five cups/1-1.25 L of coffee) increases one's total energy output by about 80 to 150 calories a day. Coffee also increases the body's use of fatty acids.

It should be remembered that the effect of caffeine depends a great deal on the individual and his or her age.

COFFEE AND OSTEOPOROSIS

Currently, the association between coffee drinking and osteoporosis, a disease most common in older women, which makes bones brittle and more porous, is still under the microscope.

Caffeine is definitely known to increase calcium excretion, and women who are heavy coffee drinkers lose more calcium, which makes them more susceptible to bone fractures and the risk of osteoporosis in their senior years. Recent studies, however, advise that drinking just one glass of milk can offset the calcium loss caused by two cups (500 mL) of coffee. Therefore, a double bone-building latte could be a woman's best friend! If a woman loves her Espresso or cappuccino, she doesn't necessarily have to part with it, however, she should try to include extra calcium-rich foods, such as yogurt, cheese and milk, in her daily diet.

A SIP TO BREATHE BETTER

Drinking coffee helps some people with asthma breath better. Caffeine belongs to the same chemical family as a medicine used to fight asthma. A specific study has demonstrated that asthma sufferers, who drink coffee regularly, show 19 percent fewer symptoms than non-coffee drinkers.

Those who suffer from asthma due to physical activity can alleviate bronchial constriction by taking a cup of coffee before beginning physical exercise. Caffeine actually dilates the bronchioles in the lungs, which help regulate the respiratory system.

My daughters, Ingrid and Krista, both of whom have suffered from asthma, claim that when their asthma was bad, they found that drinking a cup of coffee would relax them and their breathing ability would improve. Ingrid stated that when she felt "tight" due to the asthma, having a cup of coffee "to relax", gave her a positive physiological (mind to body) affect.

Once again, caffeine responses may vary from person to person.

"We'd like you to help us with a little research, Ed. We're going to measure your level of productivity after replacing all of your blood with black coffee."

*Father, if I don't drink my little cup of coffee three times a day,
I'll dry up like a piece of roast goat-flesh . . . I will sacrifice my
fashions, my walks, my ribbons – before I will sacrifice coffee.*

ADDICTION VS. PASSION

*According to the "Coffee Science Source", from the Medical Data on Coffee and Health,
an addiction is a strong dependence on a drug, characterized by three elements:*

1. *severe withdrawal symptoms;*
2. *tolerance to a given dose, or the need for more of the same substance;*
3. *the loss of control, or the need to consume the substance at all costs.*

Evidence shows that coffee drinkers do not exhibit these symptoms of addiction.

"There's the facts!" As Julia McKinnell quoted in her non-addiction article for the National
Post: "Coffee is like anything else – Brussels sprouts, celery, headcheese, a take-it-or-leave-it
thing." That is, until the aromatic kitchen roosters are switched on, hypnotizing our senses to
anticipate our first morning cups of coffee or Espresso. Is this habit an addiction or are we just
passionately dependent on our beloved brew?

In North America alone, the average caffeinated coffee consumption is about
230 milligrams (2 to 2$^1/_2$ cups/500 to 625 mL) per person per day. In general, a good majority
of the world's population needs this regular "java jolt" or "coffee fix", for one reason or another.

Serious coffee drinkers may find it difficult to "kick" the habit. Interruption of the regular
consumption of coffee may produce a classic symptom, "a splitting headache". Absence of the
caffeine fix also makes regular consumers feel irritable and tired. Relief from these withdrawal
symptoms is often the reason to continue drinking our cup(s) of coffee or Espresso. Regular
consumption of 3 cups (750 mL) a day, and upwards, causes "physical dependence" on caffeine;
its habitual intake causes the body to develop a tolerance to caffeine.

According to Time Webster's New Ideal Dictionary, *"a passion is the strong liking for some
activity, object, or concept; ardent affection; an object of desire or deep interest." Speaking for
myself, my drinking love affair with my "must-have" morning coffee is a combination of personal
passion and addiction. Good or bad, slowly sipping my favorite brew gives me permission to
celebrate my initial morning idleness, demanding no skill, no commitment and no stress! (Too
bad the rest of my day doesn't always continue like that!)*

In summary, it's all about making a simple choice, whether to drink coffee or not! Whether
to drink caffeinated or not! Then it's about setting your own boundaries as to how much you
consume if you do choose to drink coffee.

*Whether you drink it or leave it; listen to your body. Whatever you decide, take everything
in moderation and do everything with passion.*

Coffee-o-logy: A Glossary

. . . A CUP OF COFFEE
DETRACTS NOTHING FROM YOUR INTELLECT . . .

-CHARLES MAURICE DE TALLEYRAND (1754-1838), 18TH CENTURY FRENCH STATESMAN

COFFEE-O-LOGY: A GLOSSARY

PART 1
COFFEE BAR BEVERAGE TERMINOLOGY

When you enter a coffee shop or Espresso bar, the lineup of coffee bar beverage choices can be overwhelming. What is the difference between a café au lait and a cappuccino? The following guide will give you a basic understanding of Espresso-based coffee beverages and will make you a coffee pro when ordering!

AMERICANO This refers to a 6-oz. (170 mL) serving of Espresso diluted with water.

BREVE A latte made with steamed half and half instead of milk, such as a Breve latte, a Breve Mocha or a Breve cappuccino.

CAFÉ AU LAIT (or Café Con Leche) A French version of the Italian caffe latte, this is a popular French breakfast drink made up of equal amounts of freshly brewed dark roasted coffee and hot or scalded milk.

CAFFE This is the European term for a coffee (Kaffee in German). In Italy and France, if you order a "caffe" or "café" you will get an Espresso.

CAFFE LATTE A popular drink in Italy which is one-quarter freshly brewed Espresso and three-quarters hot milk. Italians do not add foamed milk, but Americans do. Italians sometimes add more steamed milk than Americans. Sometimes the drink is really served as a giant-sized cappuccino.

CAFFE MACCHIATO This drink is simply an Espresso stained or "dolloped" with about 2 tablespoons (30mL) of foamed milk.

CAFFE MOCHA This is a chocolate variation of the caffe latte. Either cocoa powder or chocolate syrup is added at the beginning of preparing the drink, the chocolate is mixed (or frothed) with hot milk until thoroughly blended, before the Espresso is added.

CAFÉ NOIR In France, this term or "Espresso Noir" is used for a single shot of Espresso.

CAFFE CON PANNA "Con panna" means "with cream" in Italian. This is simply a straight shot of Espresso topped with whipped cream instead of foamed milk.

CAFFEOL A volatile complex released by the roasting of coffee beans, which produces aroma.

CAPPUCCINO The classic choice of Espresso drinks is made with one-third Espresso, one-third steamed milk and one-third foamed milk.

CAPPUCCINO CHIARO This is a term used in Italy for a cappuccino which has less coffee and more milk.

CAPPUCCINO SCURO This is a term used in Italy for a cappuccino which has more coffee and less milk.

COWBOY COFFEE Sometimes referred to as campfire, open-pot or hobo coffee, ground coffee is steeped in boiling water and then strained in order to separate the grounds from the brew. Cowboy legend has it that the separation method was often a clean sock, into which the ground coffee was spooned before being immersed in water.

DRY CAPPUCCINO This is another version of an Espresso macchiato. It is basically an Espresso with foam on top, but no steamed milk.

ESPRESSO A dark, rich full-bodied coffee brew which is made when finely ground firmly compressed Italian or dark-roasted coffee, is packed in the portafilter of an Espresso machine and a small amount of water is forced through the coffee at about 125 pounds/60 kg of pressure per square inch/2.5 cm^2 (or 9 atmospheric pressure). The contact time between the water and the ground coffee is very brief, approximately 25 seconds. It is often served in small quantities, referred to as a "shot".

ESPRESSO ALLONGE This is a weak Espresso in France. It can also be referred to as Café Allonge.

ESPRESSO DOPPIO This is a double (two) shot of Espresso, in a 4-oz. (113 mL) cup or in a beverage.

ESPRESSO SOLO This is a single (one) shot of Espresso, served either alone or in a beverage.

FILTERED COFFEE This is an economical method of brewing coffee using filter paper to separate the coffee grounds from the soluble coffee.

FRAPPÉ This is an iced or frozen mixture or drink; a thick milkshake. Greeks are famous for their coffee-based frappés.

GRANITA This is an Italian gourmet "slushie", meaning beverages using crushed ice.

IRISH COFFEE A classic beverage made of brewed coffee, Irish whiskey, sugar and heavy cream. It is usually served in a tall glass mug with whipped cream on top.

JAVA This is a slang name for coffee. Legend has it this term came from the Indonesian island of Java. It was colonized by the Dutch in the eighteenth century, and became a successful center of coffee production.

MEXICAN COFFEE This coffee is brewed with cinnamon and brown sugar, mixed with cocoa and served hot with whipped cream on top.

MOCHACCINO This is made with freshly brewed Espresso and steamed chocolate milk in equal parts. It is topped with foam from the steamed chocolate milk.

RED EYE This is a cup of brewed coffee with a shot of Espresso – double strength!

RISTRETTO (SHORT) Deriving from the word "restricted", a regular shot of Espresso is made with less than the usual amount of hot water, essentially stopped or pulled "short"; hence sometimes referred to as "short pull". This produces an intense flavor and brings out the Espresso's caramelly sweetness.

SINGLE This is basically the same as an ESPRESSO SOLO, a single shot of Espresso.

SKINNY (TALL) Also called "twiggy", this refers to a drink, usually a tall latte, made with skim or non-fat milk.

STEAMERS (or STEAMED MILK) This is a beverage which contains no Espresso. It is heated by the injection of steam and the volume of the milk is increased. Flavored syrups, producing many flavor variations, may be added to the steamed milk.

SOYA-CCINO This is a "new-age" cappuccino using soymilk or rice milk as a milk or dairy substitute. The flavor is slightly different, but for the non-dairy coffee drinker or lactose-intolerant, both substitutes make a good alternative to a traditional cappuccino.

WET CAPPUCCINO A wet cappuccino has more steamed milk and less foam than a regular cappuccino.

PART 2
COFFEE TERMINOLOGY

Relatively small differences will be brought out in the cup, contributed by the type of coffee bean, the various coffee machines and methods used. Certain coffee terms are used in the language of coffee. The following references describe some of these: bean types, coffee-making techniques, and general barista procedures.

ARABICA COFFEE *A specific variety of coffee, one of the two main coffee species – arabica beans are considered to be the best variety of coffee. It is still the most widely grown. Arabica beans produce the best flavors since they are grown mainly at high altitudes in semitropical climates near the equator. They naturally contain about 1.1 percent caffeine; robusta beans have about 2.2 percent caffeine, double that of the arabica.*

BARISTA *A person who is a master of the Espresso machine and makes coffee as a profession.*

BLEND *A mixture of two or more varieties of coffee beans from different parts of the world, and sometimes from different roasts. A roaster usually has secret recipes from which to produce customized house blends.*

CAFFEINE *A substance naturally found in coffee that acts as a stimulant. The darker the roast, the less caffeine it contains, since caffeine burns off while the coffee is being roasted.*

CREMA *A golden tan foam which appears at the surface of a "perfectly" brewed cup of Espresso. A number of factors is crucial in achieving this; good quality and the correct amount of fresh Espresso coffee; the correct degree of pressure; the water temperature dosing the perfect-sized coffee grind; and the contact time between the water and the coffee grounds. When the coffee oils and colloids are released under pressure and come into contact with oxygen, the characteristic crema is formed on top.*

CUPPING *A scientific and ritualized process whereby coffee tasting specialists ultimately judge and evaluate samples of coffee beans considered world market purchases, keeping notes on specific characteristics of the coffees.*

DOSE *The correct amount of Espresso coffee which is dispensed from the grinder to brew one serving of Espresso coffee.*

DOLLOP *Usually a lump or blob of a soft substance. This is a term for an unmeasured amount of something, whipped cream, for example.*

DRY (WASHING) METHOD *This is one of the two methods of preparing the coffee beans after harvesting. The beans are inexpensively and ineffectively left in the sun to dry, for up to 3 weeks. "Dry" beans are less expensive and less fine than the alternate "wet" beans.*

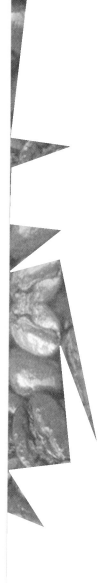

EXTRACTION RATE This is a term referring to the brewing time, and the amount of soluble solids which pass from the coffee beans to the brewed coffee, giving it body and flavor. The shorter the brewing time, the finer the grind must be, so that the extraction is quick and thorough. If the brewing time is long, then the grind should be coarse, to avoid overextracting undesirable substances.

FAIR TRADE COFFEE This is coffee produced by coffee growers, usually subsistence growers, who have been paid a reasonable price for their coffee, based on an economic formula (see page 179) rather than the pennies per pound they usually receive.

FOAMED MILK This is the term given to milk which has been both heated and aerated with hot steam. The ideal consistency of foamed milk is thick and frothy, a very lightly whipped texture that holds its shape and can be sculpted. It differs from STEAMED MILK in that foamed milk usually doubles in volume, whereas the steamed milk remains unchanged.

FRENCH PRESS See *PLUNGER POT*.

GREEN COFFEE Unroasted coffee is called "green".

GRINDING This is the process of pulverizing coffee beans (after they have been roasted) to various sizes to suit the coffee brewing technique being used.

HARD BEAN This describes coffee grown at relatively high altitudes, 4,000 to 4,500 feet (1,200 to 1,372 metres). Coffee grown above 4,500 feet (1,372 metres) is referred to as strictly hard bean. These beans mature more slowly and are harder and denser, making them more desirable.

HARMLESS This is a term used sometimes by baristas, referring to a coffee beverage that has been made with skim milk, and decaf Espresso or decaf coffee.

INFUSION When heated water passes through coffee grounds, extracting the soluble coffee, this process is called infusion.

ORGANIC COFFEES These coffees are certified by independent agencies as organically grown, processed, stored and roasted. This means that no synthetic chemical pesticides, fertilizers, cleaners, etc., have come into contact with the coffee trees or beans. Organic coffees cost more than similar non-organic coffees due to higher costs of production and the additional costs of certification.

PLUNGER POT This may also be referred to as a French Press, after the French manufacturer. Coffee grounds steep in hot water in the pot, and then a fine metal screen is pressed down through the liquid to separate the grounds from the brewed coffee. This brew is the next thickest textured coffee to professional Espresso or the Espresso stovetop method.

PUMP MACHINE This is an Espresso brewer which produces high pressure, using a small electric pump. It uses the high pressure to force hot but not boiling water through finely ground Espresso. Most quality home Espresso machines include a pump.

ROBUSTA One of the two main coffee species, it is responsible for the strength and intensity of the coffee. It lacks the aroma and smoothness of its competitor, the arabica coffee bean. It grows well at low altitudes, and has twice the amount of caffeine, about 2.2 percent of the arabica bean, which has about 1.1 percent.

SHADE-GROWN COFFEE This coffee is literally "made-in-the-shade". It refers to a method of growing coffee in a natural environment including shade trees and songbirds. Proponents of this product say that growing coffee in this manner will protect the natural rain forests and protect certain animal species.

SOFT BEAN COFFEE Describes coffee grown at relatively low altitudes (under 4,000 feet/1,200 metres). Beans grown at lower altitudes mature more quickly and produce a lighter, more porous coffee bean.

SPECIALTY COFFEE This can refer to custom whole-bean coffees sold by the country of origins, roasting styles, sometimes with additional flavors. In the general public, this term is also being used to refer to fancy coffees, for example cappuccinos, mochaccino, etc.

SPENT GROUNDS This refers to used ground coffee; it is very good for composting.

STEAM WAND This is the tube attached to home and professional Espresso machines. High-pressured steam is delivered out of the end of the wand. It is used mainly to make steamed and foamed milk.

STEAMED MILK This is milk which has been heated by steam. Its volume remains unchanged, unlike that of foamed milk where the volume of the milk is usually doubled.

TAMPER This is a small tool which is used to press or "tamp down" the surface of the ground coffee in the metal filter holder of an Espresso machine. A tamper almost always has a flat bottom, and is slightly narrower than the filter.

THERMAL CARAFE Best known as a "thermos", this insulated container is the ideal way to store brewed coffee. The flavor of the coffee in a tightly sealed carafe, can remain intact for up to an hour. Keeping coffee on a burner for any length of time, produces a sour, bitter brew.

STRENGTH In coffee, strength does not refer to flavor. It refers to the ratio of coffee to water. The brew is stronger with more coffee grounds to less water.

SWISS-WATER DECAFFEINATION PROCESS This refers to a specific method of removing the caffeine from coffee beans. In this process, a charcoal filter is used to remove the caffeine, never chemicals. Chemicals are sometimes used in the "water decaffeination process".

WET (WASHING) METHOD This is one of the two methods of drying beans after harvesting. This method is more efficient and more expensive than the alternative drying method. Washed coffees are finer and more expensive than "dry" coffees.

WATER DECAFFEINATION PROCESS In this method of decaffeination, all the caffeine and soluble solids are removed from green coffee beans by soaking them in water. The water process can involve chemicals at certain stages.

All the world eats and drinks, but few can distinguish flavors.
-TSE-TZE, *THE BOOK OF THE MEAN* (5TH CENTURY BC)

PART 3
COFFEE-TASTING TERMINOLOGY

The way people "talk" about coffee, and how coffee "tastes", may sometimes sound like a foreign language. Fortunately, we all share a common set of taste perceptions. It is on this basis that the following vocabulary is built. These terms describe taste characteristics associated with and deriving from the coffee bean itself. **"HAPPY TASTING!"**

ACIDITY Flavorful acids form when coffee is being roasted, giving the coffee life and zip. Roasting eliminates some of the coffee beans' acidity, so the lighter the roast, the more the acids – the result is a sharper tasting coffee. Very dark roasts destroy most acids and will taste dull and flat. This does not refer to bitterness.

AFTERTASTE The sensation of brewed coffee remaining in the mouth after swallowing is aftertase. I have always professed that a superior Espresso coffee should have a lingering aftertaste sensation on the palate, for about 10 to 15 minutes after swallowing, leaving an almost nutty flavor, NEVER bitter!

AGED Green coffee beans which have been stored in a typically hot and humid climate for a year or two before being shipped are called aged. Aged coffee has a soft, mellow flavor and heavy body. Aged beans are expensive, because stocks are tied up. They are sought mainly for blends.

AROMA The scent or smell of freshly brewed coffee is its aroma. It may be described as "strong", "rich", "delicate", "moderate", "faint", "fragrant", "pungent", or "bitter".

BALANCE The satisfying presence of all the basic taste characteristics, where none overpowers another, is the balance.

BLAND This flavor ranges from soft to neutral. It is most common in arabica coffee beans, which are generally associated with the smoothness, roundedness and body of the coffee.

BITTER The worst enemy of the Espresso bean is the unpleasant flavor of an over-roasted, over-extracted "burnt brew". This harsh sensation which can leave the mouth in a "puckered position" is largely due to the roasting technology of the coffee bean. If the beans have been left in the roasters too long, the gravity effect on the beans can cause them to "burn" on the walls of the roasting bins, creating a coffee which is burnt, blackened and bitter! "Air-roasting" is a process which never burns the beans.

BODY This tasting term best describes the texture and sensation of coffee in the mouth; the weight of coffee on the palate. Coffee may feel "strong", "full", "heavy" or "light", "thin" or even "syrupy".

CARAMELLY This descriptive term to the "caramelization" of the coffee bean in the roasting process. The darker the bean, the higher the degree of caramelization which has taken place when the beans were heated. Beans are naturally high in carbohydrates, which must be heated to develop toasty sweet flavors. Caramelized sugars give body and mouth feel to a darker roast. When caramelization is taken too far, the coffee will taste burnt.

DELICATE Characterized by a fragile, subtle flavor, related to "mellow", it is perceived by the tip of the tongue.

EARTHY A more generalized term describing an unclean taste that reminds one of eating dirt, it is a tasting term for "low-grade" or "dirty" coffee made with poor processing methods.

EXOTIC An unusual or unexpected aroma and flavor, this is used to describe coffees which are sweet and spicy, especially those from East Africa and Indonesia.

FLAVOR The sensation experienced when tasting coffee. It is the total perception of acidity, aroma and body.

HARSH This term is used to describe an irritating, rough, or unpleasant sharpness in the coffee.

LIGHT A qualitative term to describe aroma, acidity, and body, "light" coffee may have a fine, delicate flavor or be lacking aroma, acidity or body.

MALTY This aromatic sensation produces a taste or smell that reminds one of toasted grains.

MELLOW A term for a well-balanced full-flavor coffee that has a smooth, rounded taste; a mellow coffee generally lacks acidity. It may also be called "soft".

MILD This is a business term for all arabica coffees, describing a coffee that is delicate in flavor, but is not harsh or unpleasant.

MUSTY This flavor is caused by either overheating or improper drying or aging of the coffee beans.

NUTTY This aromatic vapor is left on the palate once the coffee is swallowed. It is characteristic of a quality Espresso which is not bitter.

RICH This term is used for coffees offering an intense depth and complexity, pleasant body, flavor and aroma.

SOFT This is a taste referring to a coffee low in acidity, mellow or sweet.

SOUR This undesirable sharp, acid-like taste results from under-ripe, fermented beans.

SPICY This term refers to the aroma or flavor of a coffee suggestive of spices.

STALE An unpleasant flavor, it is the aroma of a roasted coffee which has gone beyond its prime and has oxidized.

STRONG A tasting term referring to the intensity and assertive strength in the coffee, not to be confused with bitterness. Strong is usually used to describe a robusta coffee. Robusta coffee beans are grown at lower altitudes and, therefore, generally receive more sun than the higher-quality, milder arabica coffee beans which are grown at higher altitudes.

SWEET This describes coffee which is free from any bitterness and has a pleasant, smooth taste with a clean flavor.

TANGY This denotes a zesty pleasant flavor.

WILD This denotes a pungent vigorous flavor.

WINEY A term used to characterize a full-bodied "well-matured" smooth coffee. it is reminiscent of high-quality, high-altitude-grown arabica coffees.

. . . by coffee you get upon leaving the table;
a mind full of wisdom, thoughts lucid . . .
-AUTHOR UNKNOWN, EXCERPTED FROM AN 8TH CENTURY FRENCH POEM

KAFFEEKLATSCH (COFFEE TALK) TRIVIA

Coffee is one of the world's top three most popular beverages, alongside water and tea.

Coffee is second to oil (petroleum), in terms of dollars traded worldwide. Total world green (unroasted) coffee trade is valued at $14 billion annually.

Coffee is a giant global industry, employing more than 20 million people.

World coffee production estimates for the year 2000 will total 102.5 million, 60 kilogram (132 lb.) bags, according to the latest report from the Association of Coffee Producing Countries (ACPC).

Brazil and Colombia are the world's two main suppliers of coffee, with Brazil supplying 30 percent of the global coffee supply.

The first recorded consumption of coffee by humans was in A.D. 575.

Coffee trees are self-pollinating, and have been successfully transplanted all over the world. Plantation coffee trees have been known to bear fruit (coffee cherries) when over 100 years old.

Plantation coffee trees are at their harvesting prime at 10 to 15 years old, however, on the average, they live 25 to 40 years old.

Arabica coffee trees are an evergreen and grow to heights of 14 to 20 (4.3 to 6 metres), however, they are pruned and kept to 8 to 10 feet (2.5 to 3 metres) to simplify harvesting.

Coffee "cherries" on the same tree ripen or mature at different times, which is why they are picked predominantly by hand; coffee-harvesting remains virtually untouched by mechanization.

Coffee is the seed of a cherry (or berry) harvested from trees which grow in a subtropical belt around the world. These trees are only native to Ethiopia and Yemen.

Each coffee cherry yields two coffee beans.

Five pounds (approximately 2,000 units) of coffee cherries, from a coffee tree, will produce a single pound of green (unroasted) coffee beans.

The finest coffees and Espresso blends are made from arabica coffee beans, and all specialty coffees come from the arabica bean.

It takes approximately 42 coffee beans to make an average serving of Espresso coffee.

Every cup of coffee which is consumed requires 1.4 square feet (0.427 metres^2) of coffee-cultivated land.

The average coffee tree produces only one to two pounds (500 g to 1 kg) of roasted coffee per year, and takes up to four to five years to produce its first crop.

Two pounds (1 kg) of roasted coffee requires 4,000 to 5,000 coffee beans.

A pound (500 g) of coffee yields about 40 cups of coffee.

The amount of caffeine in coffee beans varies by the type of coffee tree species. Robusta coffee beans, which are responsible for the intensity and strength of the coffee, contain approximately 2 to 4.5 percent caffeine; arabica coffee beans, which are responsible for the aroma and body of the coffee, contain 1 to 1.7 percent caffeine.

Well-stored, roasted, whole coffee beans will keep their flavor and aroma for a week.

Ground coffee beans go stale in a few hours. The greatest contaminants to ground coffee are light, heat and oxygen.

In Italy, coffee and Espresso have the same meaning. Espresso is considered so essential in Italy, the government regulates its price.

Italy now has over 200,000 Espresso bars. In Italy, a barista holds a respected position.

Ninety percent of the Espresso consumed in Italy is straight, with or without sugar. The remaining ten percent is consumed cappuccino style.

Some general coffee culture drinking habits:
> Italians drink their Espresso with sugar;
> Germans and the Swiss drink coffee with equal parts hot chocolate;
> Mexicans – with cinnamon;
> Belgians – with chocolate;
> Ethiopians – with a pinch of salt;
> Moroccans – with peppercorns;
> Middle Easterners – add cardamom and spices to their coffee.

Whipped cream is the favorite coffee addition amongst Austrians.

"Kaffee Schnufflers" were a special government force hired to sniff out illicit coffee roasters and smugglers in Germany during the late 1700s.

In Greece and Turkey, it is customary that the eldest is always served coffee first.

In the Middle East, it is customary today, as it was five centuries ago, that women are not accepted in coffee houses. Only a few major cities catering to tourists admit women today.

In Arabic, the creamy foam of a strong coffee is called the "wesh", meaning "the face of the coffee" and to serve it with no foam is to "lose face"!!

Today, the World Health Organization defines coffee as "a non-nutritive dietary component". It is not considered as a food, even though it does contain some nutrients such as niacin.

The International Olympic Committee lists coffee/caffeine as a prohibited substance, and screen Olympic athletes for excess amounts of caffeine in their bodies. Athletes who test positive for more than 12 micrograms of caffeine per milliliter of urine may be disqualified from the Olympic Games. This level may be reached after drinking about 5 cups of coffee.

During the American Civil War, soldiers were offered a choice as part of their personal rations: either eight pounds (4.5 kg) of ground roasted coffee, or ten pounds of green coffee beans.

Following World War II, US studies found that 10,000 marriages a year could be directly traced back to a shared coffee break.

During the war, businesses found they could increase office work productivity by introducing what came to be called the "coffee break".

The first recorded use of the word "cappuccino" in English was in 1948, in a published work about San Francisco.

Espresso coffee contains over 600 chemical compositions: sugars, caffeine, proteins in solution, emulsion of coffee oils, colloids and coffee particles in suspension with tiny gas bubbles.

"Joe" is a nineteenth century American slang term for coffee.

"Cup of Joe" is a term which is still used in coffee society today. Legend has it that the US Navy Admiral "Joe" Daniels, on becoming Chief of Naval Operations, outlawed alcohol on board ships, except for special occasions. Coffee then became the beverage of choice, and was named in his honor. Hence, the term "cup of Joe".

Coffee consumers are choosing to drink better coffee, purchasing coffee products with a focus on quality, and demanding a variety of coffees to suit their palates, rather than choosing price-based products.

According to the Specialty Coffee Association of America's 1999 Coffee Market Summary, 47 percent of the American population drink Espresso, cappuccino, latte, or iced/cold coffees, as compared to the 1997 summary (two years earlier) showing 35 percent of the population consuming these types of beverages – an increase of 28 million drinkers in just one year!

A "latte" laugh at a South London coffee-pub: a young barmaid claimed that drinking a dozen cups of cappuccino a day made her breasts grow by 3 "cup" sizes. Her pub customers jokingly said that she must be drinking "Breastcafés"!

YOU KNOW YOU'RE A JAVA JUNKIE WHEN . . .

. . . Starbucks owns the mortgage on your house.

. . . Your first-aid kit contains two pints of coffee with an I.V. hook-up.

. . . You think CPR stands for "Coffee Provides Resuscitation."

. . . The nurse needs a scientific calculator to take your pulse.

. . . You soak your dentures in coffee overnight.

. . . Instant coffee takes too long.

. . . You don't even wait for the water to boil anymore.

. . . The Taster's Choice couple wants to adopt you.

. . . All your kids are named "Joe!".

. . . You name your cats "Cream and Sugar".

. . . You spend every vacation visiting "Maxwell House".

. . . Your lips are permanently stuck in the sipping position.

. . . Your taste buds are so numb, you could drink your lava lamp.

. . . You've worn out the handle on your favorite mug.

. . . You have a picture of your coffee mug on your coffee mug.

. . . You want to come back as a coffee mug in your next life.

. . . You go to sleep just so you can wake up and smell the coffee.

. . . You sleep with your eyes open.

. . . You haven't blinked since the last lunar eclipse.

. . . You speed walk in your sleep.

. . . You can outlast the Energizer bunny.

. . . People can test their batteries in your ears.

. . . You short out motion detectors.

. . . Your three favorite things in life are . . . coffee before, coffee during and after.

. . . The only time you're standing still is during an earthquake.

. . . You have to watch videos in fast-forward.

. . . You call radio talk shows and they ask you to turn yourself down.

. . . You can take a picture of yourself from ten feet away without using the timer.

. . . You get a speeding ticket even when you're parked.

. . . You can jump-start your car without cables.

. . . Your thermos is on wheels.

. . . You have a bumper sticker that says" "Coffee drinkers are good in the sack".

. . . You're the employee of the month at the local coffeehouse, and you don't even work there!

. . . You've built a miniature city out of little plastic stirrers.

. . . You can type sixty words per minute . . . with your feet.

. . . You chew on other people's fingernails.

. . . You're so jittery that people use your hands to blend their margaritas.

. . . Your nervous twitch registers on the Richter scale.

. . . You don't need a hammer to pound nails.

. . . People get dizzy just watching you.

. . . You channel surf faster without a remote.

. . . You walk twenty miles on your treadmill before you realize it's not plugged in.

. . . You don't sweat, you percolate.

. . . You've worn out your third pair of tennis shoes this week.

. . . You think being called a "drip" is a compliment.

. . . You don't get mad, you get steamed.

. . . You buy "half and half" by the barrel.

. . . Your coffee mug is insured by Lloyd's of London.

In every country in the world "coffee" is pronounced similarly,
except for Egypt and Armenia!

THE FINAL WORD ON COFFEE: A GLOBAL TRANSLATION

AMHARIC ....Bunn

ARABIC ....Qahwa

BASQUE ....Kaffia

BRETON ....Kafe

BOHEMIAN ....Kava

CANTONESE ....Kia-fey

CZECH ....Kava

DANISH ....Kaffe

DUTCH ....Koffie

EGYPTIAN ....Masbout

ESPERANTO ....Kafo

FINNISH....................Kahvi

FRENCH ....Café

GERMAN ....Kaffee

GREEK ....Kafes

HAWAIIAN ....Kope

HEBREW ....Kaffee

HINDU ....Coffee

HUNGARIAN............Kave

INDONESIAN ....Kope

INUIT.........................Kaufee

IRANIAN ....Gehve

ITALIAN ....Caffe

JAPANESE ....Koohii

KHMER ....Gafe

LAOTIAN ....Kafe

LATIN ....Cofea

MALAYAN ....Kawa, Koppi

MANDARIN ....Kafei

NORWEGIAN ....Kaffe

POLISH ....Kawa

PORTUGESE ....Cafe

RUSSIAN..................Kafe

RUMANIAN ....Cafea

SERBO-CROATIAN....Kafe

SPANISH ....Cafe

SWAHILI....................Kahawa

TAGALOG ....Kape

THAI ....Kafe

TURKISH ....Kahve

YIDDISH....................Kave

BIBLIOGRAPHY

Castle, Timothy James. *The Perfect Cup.*
    Reading, Massachussets: Perseus Books (Addison Wesley), 1991.

Coffee and Beverage Magazine, Spring Volume 1998.

CoffeeTALK Magazine, November 1995.

Davids, Kenneth. *A Guide to Buying, Brewing and Enjoying.*
    Singapore: 101 Productions, 1991.

Davids, Kenneth. *Espresso: Ultimate Coffee.*
    Santa Rosa: Cole Group, 1993.

Dicum, Gregory and N. Lullinger. *The Coffee Book*, 1999.

Freshcup Magazine.

Illy, Francesco and Ricardo. *The Book of Coffee: A Gourmet's Guide.*
    Milan: Mondadori, 1989 - 1st ed. New York: Abbeville Press, 1992.

Kummer, Corby. *The Joy of Coffee: The Essential Guide to Buying, Brewing and Enjoying.* Shelburne, VT: Chapters Publishing, 1995.

Lacalamita, Tom. *The Ultimate Espresso Machine Cookbook.*
    Simon and Shuster, 1995.

Lavazza. *Guida al Caffé.*
    Milan: Centro Luigi Lavazza, 1991.

Roden, Claudia. *Coffee, A Coffee Lover's Companion*, 1999.
    Pavillion Book, London, England.

Rolnick Harry. *The Complete Book of Coffee.*
    Hong Kong: Melitta, 1982.

Specialty Coffee Retailer: June 1998, April 1998.

Tea and Coffee Trade Journal:
    November 1996, Volume 168/No.11.
    May 1997, Volume 169/No. 5
    July 1997, Volume 169/No. 7.
    July 1998, Volume 170/No. 7.
    April 1998, Volume 170/No. 4.

Hot Cappuccino Cocktails

Iced Cappuccino Cocktails

Holiday Cappuccino Cocktails

Coffee Syrups

Whipped Creams

GENERAL INDEX

A GREAT GIFT IDEA

ORDER BY PHONE (24 HOURS) 1-877-888-8898
OR
ORDER BY FAX 1-403-873-1005 USING THIS FORM
OR
ORDER ONLINE: www.CappuccinoCocktails.com
(Look for special offers only online)

PLEASE SEND _____ **COPIES OF "CAPPUCCINO COCKTAILS"** @ *$19.95 each (US $16.95).*

$ _____ – *Total cost for "CAPPUCCINO COCKTAILS" books @ $19.95 each (US $16.95).*

$ _____ – *Add $5.00 (each book), for shipping and handling.*

$ _____ – *Add $10.00 (each book), for international orders.*

$ _____ – *Sub-Total*

$ _____ – *Add 7% GST (Canadian orders only). Prices subject to change.*

$ _____ – ***TOTAL***

METHOD OF PAYMENT:

(Payable to ESP Publishing Inc.)

CHARGE TO: ❑ *VISA* ❑ *MASTERCARD* ❑ *CHECK OR MONEY ORDER ENCLOSED*

credit card number   *expiry date*

_____   _____

Name on credit card (please print)   *Purchaser's Signature*

SOLD TO: **SHIP TO:**

Name: _____   *Name:* _____

Address: _____   *Address:* _____

City: _____   *City:* _____

Prov/State _____   *Prov/State* _____

Postal/Zip Code _____   *Postal/Zip Code* _____

*Telephone (   ) _____   **Telephone (   )* _____

*In case we have a question about your order.

Please allow 2 to 3 weeks for delivery.

ESP PUBLISHING INC. - CAPPUCCINO COCKTAILS
4620 Manilla Road SE, Calgary, Alberta Canada T2G 4B7 Tel: (403) 830-8086 Fax: (403) 873-1005

A GREAT GIFT IDEA

ORDER BY PHONE (24 HOURS) 1-877-888-8898
OR
ORDER BY FAX 1-403-873-1005 USING THIS FORM
OR
ORDER ONLINE: www.CappuccinoCocktails.com
(Look for special offers only online)

PLEASE SEND _____ COPIES OF "CAPPUCCINO COCKTAILS" @ $19.95 each (US $16.95).

$ _____ – Total cost for "CAPPUCCINO COCKTAILS" books @ $19.95 each (US $16.95).

$ _____ – Add $5.00 (each book), for shipping and handling.

$ _____ – Add $10.00 (each book), for international orders.

$ _____ – Sub-Total

$ _____ – Add 7% GST (Canadian orders only). Prices subject to change.

$ _____ – TOTAL

METHOD OF PAYMENT:

(Payable to ESP Publishing Inc.)

CHARGE TO: ❏ *VISA* ❏ *MASTERCARD* ❏ *CHECK OR MONEY ORDER ENCLOSED*

credit card number ⬚⬚⬚⬚⬚⬚⬚⬚⬚⬚⬚⬚⬚⬚⬚ ⬚⬚ - ⬚⬚ *expiry date*

Name on credit card (please print) _____

Purchaser's Signature _____

SOLD TO:

Name: _____

Address: _____

City: _____

Prov/State _____

Postal/Zip Code _____

*Telephone (   ) _____

SHIP TO:

Name: _____

Address: _____

City: _____

Prov/State _____

Postal/Zip Code _____

*Telephone (   ) _____

*In case we have a question about your order.

Please allow 2 to 3 weeks for delivery.

ESP PUBLISHING INC. - CAPPUCCINO COCKTAILS

620 Manilla Road SE, Calgary, Alberta Canada T2G 4B7 Tel: (403) 830-8086 Fax: (403) 873-1005